Praise for
No Horizon Is So Far

"If you think you know the story of the first female crossing of Antarctica, think again. More hard work, more sweat
and tears went into this historic expedition than any of
us realized. Ann and Liv are truly inspirational. Their accomplishment proves that nothing is beyond our wildest dreams."
—Billie Jean King

"Ann and Liv's historic Polar expedition is an awesome
accomplishment, but as this book shows, their work as
teachers has also had a profound impact: they inspire young
girls and boys alike to follow their dreams."
—Will Steger, world-renowned polar explorer and
  bestselling author of *North to the Pole*

PENGUIN BOOKS

NO HORIZON IS SO FAR

Liv Arnesen and Ann Bancroft are two of the world's most preeminent explorers.

In 1994, Liv Arnesen made international headlines by becoming the first woman to ski solo and unsupported to the South Pole, a fifty-day expedition of 745 miles. She wrote a book about that solo experience that was a bestseller in her native Norway. She lives outside of Oslo.

Ann Bancroft is the first woman in history to cross the ice to both the North and South poles. In 1995 she was inducted into the National Women's Hall of Fame. She lives outside of St. Paul, Minnesota.

Cheryl Dahle is a writer based in San Francisco. Her work has appeared in *Fast Company* and *Working Mother,* among other publications.

NO HORIZON

IS SO FAR

*Two Women and Their Historic
Journey Across Antarctica*

LIV ARNESEN AND ANN BANCROFT

with Cheryl Dahle

PENGUIN BOOKS

PENGUIN BOOKS

Published by the Penguin Group
Penguin Group (USA) Inc., 375 Hudson Street, New York, New York 10014, U.S.A.
Penguin Books Ltd, 80 Strand, London WC2R 0RL, England
Penguin Books Australia Ltd, 250 Camberwell Road,
    Camberwell, Victoria 3124, Australia
Penguin Books Canada Ltd, 10 Alcorn Avenue, Toronto, Ontario, Canada M4V 3B2
Penguin Books India (P) Ltd, 11 Community Centre,
    Panchsheel Park, New Delhi – 110 017, India
Penguin Group (NZ), cnr Airborne and Rosedale Roads,
    Albany, Auckland 1310, New Zealand
Penguin Books (South Africa) (Pty) Ltd, 24 Sturdee Avenue,
    Rosebank, Johannesburg 2196, South Africa

Penguin Books Ltd, Registered Offices: 80 Strand, London WC2R 0RL, England

First published in the United States of America by Da Capo Press,
a member of Perseus Book Group 2003
Published in Penguin Books 2004

10 9 8 7 6 5 4 3 2 1

Excerpt from *Kitchen Table Wisdom* by Rachel Naomi Remen, M. D.,
copyright © 1996 by Rachel Naomi Remen, M. D. Used by permission
of Riverhead Books, an imprint of Penguin Group (USA) Inc.

CIP data available
ISBN 0-7382-0794-2 (hc.)
ISBN 0 14 30.3424 3 (pbk.)

Printed in the United States of America
Set in Bembo
Designed by Jeff Williams

I learned to wander. I learned what every dreaming child needs to know—that no horizon is so far that you cannot get above it or beyond it.

— BERYL MARKHAM
1902–1986, female English aviator, first person to fly solo across the Atlantic Ocean from London to North America

~ ANN

To Pam, my muse and my partner in all things:
truly, madly, deeply. And to our team in Minnesota
who helped bring dream to reality. You are more than
colleagues; you are family. Thank you for your passion,
energy, and friendship. Also, to the three million children,
teachers and others who followed our journey.
You gave soul and purpose to the journey that
continue to sustain us.

~ LIV

To Einar, my love.
And to the people of *yourexpedition*:
Your relentless efforts at raising funds, planning,
and supporting the Antarctic journey were
the winds in the sail of the dream that Ann and I shared.
And for the children, who made our journey worthwhile.

~ CHERYL

To my mother, whose strength and resilience inspire me.

CONTENTS

1   Hell   *1*

2   Sister Souls   *11*

3   A Path Paved with Ice and Money   *33*

4   "Send Rescue"   *55*

5   Waiting   *67*

6   Underway, Overwhelmed   *95*

7   Push to the Pole   *129*

8   Titan Dome   *161*

9   Beyond Endurance   *179*

10   End of the Journey   *191*

11   A Narrow Escape   *203*

Route Maps   *223*

Epilogue   *225*

The Equipment List   *241*

Acknowledgments   *247*

About yourexpedition   *253*

NO HORIZON IS SO FAR

chapter one

HELL

Every expedition has a reckoning point, the moment when an adventurer must navigate her own inner tumult and find strength to continue. Sometimes, discovering the will to go on is not a single event, but an equation that must be calculated with each footfall on a given trek. The true journey of any expedition is the journey of the mind. Navigating that terrain depends not on physical skill or muscle, but on character. Where one finds that hidden reserve of motivation is a litmus test of human nature. Does it come from the thirst for fame? Love of family or competition? Or from the beauty of the very terrain that might prove deadly? Because the will to continue isn't about choosing reasons to take the next one hundred steps; it's about connecting with the forces that give one's life meaning, that which one values above all else. Success on an expedition (as in life) isn't about brute strength, or even endurance, but resilience: the ability to remind oneself, over and over, of the joy of living, even amid the greatest hardship.

On February 7, 2001, having traveled more than two-thirds of the way toward their goal of traversing the continent, Ann and Liv had reached one of those reckoning points.

ANN

I was as close as I'd ever been to breaking, emotionally and physically. My knees ached so badly that I wanted to groan out loud with each step. The pain had become a constant presence, often causing tears that froze inside my goggles. The temperature hovered at −15°F (−26.1°C), but the harsh wind made it feel much colder. Exposed human flesh here would freeze in less than a minute. I longed for the relative warmth of the Minnesota winter I was missing back home. The Antarctic cold tortured the new pink skin on my cheeks, peeled raw by the intense sun and bitter wind. But at least I could still feel my feet. And how. With each downhill step, my toes jammed into the ends of my boots. I knew from experience that when I pulled off my socks that night, my toes would be purpled knobs. I would lose all my blackened toenails in a few days. Still, that was better than frostbite.

I wanted to put on my skis, but the ice was too rough and slippery here. Instead, I wore metal spikes—crampons— strapped to my boot soles for better footing. Both Liv and I had walked more than eight hours so far that day, dragging our 250-pound (113-kg) supply sleds behind us. We'd traveled less than 7 agonizing miles (11 km). On good days, when there was enough wind to use our sails and skis, we might gain 60 miles (97 km) or more in a day. Not today. Just the previous night I had written this in my journal: "Despite the pain from injury, it seems doable today! I feel as if I can endure. We will make it!" How things had changed in just twelve hours.

This was supposed to be the *easy* part of the journey. We were on the Shackleton Glacier, a frozen river of ice named for the very polar explorer who had inspired both of us as lit- tle girls. I was twelve years old when I'd first read the story of Ernest Shackleton. That brave expedition leader failed in his attempt to cross Antarctica in 1914 but did not lose the life of a single man in his command through more than a year of liv- ing on the ice and a daring sail for help. His inspiring drama, played out decades ago on this frigid, icy stage, had led me to seek out the same path—not to explore, as this continent was discovered long ago—but to journey inside myself. To see what I had to offer in this incredible test of mental strength and physical skill. It seemed that just as Shackleton had been the one to launch my dream of crossing Antarctica, the glacier named after him might be the end of it.

I'd been counting the miles to this glacier for weeks, thinking that once we arrived there, we would find smooth snow and a gentle downhill grade. We hoped, too, that the wind would pick up so that we could ski-sail across the final miles. But the Shackleton was proving to be one of the most punishing landscapes of the trip.

Until now, we'd seen plenty of crevasses, giant cracks in the ice that can widen into gaps that go down hundreds of feet, even miles, below the surface. But here, the crevasses were gullies, trenches, craters. They were wider than the 6-foot-length (1.8 m) of our fiberglass sleds, the ice ridges between them barely a few feet wide. Avoiding these crevasses was like trying to hop from rock to rock across a river without falling in the water. Except our "rocks" were made of slick ice and our "river" was a sheer drop-off of at least 12 feet (4 m) in many places. We kept leaping from ridge to ridge, hoping all the while that the terrain would get better. At least once or twice every few minutes one of our sleds slid into a crevasse. Sometimes we could tug them out alone, but more often than not, one of us would have to unhitch from her own sled and help the other pull out the errant sled. We were battling for every inch. And the flat light and vast distance of Antarctica played tricks on our eyes. The ice just ahead would tantaliz-ingly appear to flatten out, but as we came upon it, we found it just as turbulent as the trenches we'd just struggled across.

I could see Liv was in pain as well. One fingertip on her right hand had turned yellow on its way to frostbite. She had soaked her fingers in her oatmeal that morning in an attempt to get some feeling back into them. But her mood was worse than her physical condition. She didn't seem to care that the ice had torn a gash in the side of her sled. I could see one of the food bags through the hole.

We both felt the time pressure. We had only fifteen days to finish our trek across Antarctica before we were scheduled to meet our ship in McMurdo Sound. In that time, we still had more than 500 miles (805 km) to cover. Pushing beyond our cutoff date would mean stretching the trip into the beginning of the Antarctic winter, when the weather would become too dangerous for us and for the ship. Already, the windows of respite between the blizzard-like conditions were narrowing. If we had hit Shackleton glacier even a few days earlier, when the snow and wind had whirled until all visibility was gone, we could easily have fallen into one of these crevasses and broken legs, arms, or worse.

We simply had to go faster. And that would be impossible unless the ice smoothed out. Unless the wind picked up. Unless, unless, unless. This trip was starting to feel doomed. It seemed we hadn't had a break in our bad luck at any point in the journey.

Crunch! I felt something snap under my right foot. My crampon had broken. Now I would have to stop and spend precious time to fix it, if that were even possible. I called to Liv, who was a few steps ahead of me, and we both stopped for a meal break. Even with our many layers and windproof parkas, within a few minutes we would go from sweating from exertion to shivering with cold.

We drank thermoses of hot sports drink and ate chocolate in exhausted silence. I thought about the schoolgirls we had met in South Africa before starting our trek, the Norwegian kids writing letters to our base camp in Minneapolis, the children in Ecuador who were running every day, trying to add up their miles to total the length of our journey as a way of traveling with us. The image in my head of the hopeful faces of the children excited by our expedition had propelled me across the first 1,000 miles (1,610 km) of ice. Now, they haunted me. Our team back at base camp had told us that more than 3 million kids were tracking our journey on our Web site, listening to our recorded voices giving updates by satellite phone and following the online curriculum we developed. How could I tell those kids that I just couldn't make it? The very point of the trip had been to show them that dreams can become reality. What kind of message would I be sending them if I failed in my lifelong dream to cross Antarctica? I had been fundraising and planning and believing for eleven years. This was my last chance. And it now seemed that I might not make it after all. The thought of disappointing all those kids put a knot in my chest that hurt more than my knees.

LIV

I was sure that Ann was furious with me. It had been my suggestion to trek closer to the moraine of the glacier, closer to the edge, where I had thought it might be smoother. I was wrong. We had wound up in an area even worse than where we had started. We were stuck in a place where two other glaciers met the Shackleton. If these glaciers melted completely, the area would be churning with waves and rapids. The same forces were present, except that the turbulence was frozen. Everywhere we looked, the ice rivers were colliding, slowly grinding against each other and the ground.

Before our trip began, I had talked to the Australians who had traveled in the opposite direction up this glacier two years ago. When they traversed it in November, early summer in Antarctica, everything we were seeing had been covered with snow many layers thick. And heading uphill provides a clearer picture of the terrain that lies ahead. Ann and I were the only living beings to navigate *down* the glacier. We were arriving at the end of the Antarctic summer, when twenty-four hours of sunshine had been melting this place for three months. It had changed dramatically.

Still, I was annoyed with myself for picking this path, frustrated that we were losing too much time, and, most of all, I was sick of my sled. The tow bar, a short ladder section made from titanium meant to keep the sled in line at a set distance behind me, had broken shortly after we began our trek, so I was pulling my sled with a rope. There was nothing to stop the sled from drifting from side-to-side or crashing into me. When I headed downhill, my sled came chasing after me and slammed into my legs if I did not leap out of the way fast enough. I started to think of the sled as a living thing, an animal stalking me, waiting for my weak moments. Sometimes, I could feel it shimmying behind me, jerking against the rope like a wild horse. I became very good at hearing the sound of the runners skittering on the ice as the sled attacked. I could tell whether it was coming from my left or right, and then *jump!*—just as it was about to hit me. Beaten, it would slide past sullenly to wait for its next chance to push me into a crevasse. I wanted so badly just to let the damned thing fall into one. I kept thinking how satisfying it would be to listen as it shattered into thousands of pieces. I began to think about just letting it go; but instead of following that negative thought, I remembered the good things the sled contained, items that had sustained me for so many days: my fleece jacket, my warm down sleeping bag, the stove, and all the cups of hot chocolate. Not to mention the tent!

We walked on for two more hours after Ann had fixed her crampon. Then we stopped for a scheduled interview with CNN on the satellite phone; but there was breaking news, so our interview was bumped. It was funny to think that the rest of the world was so accessible to us through this modern technology, and yet, if Ann or I were to be injured in this area, no plane could land here to save us. The terrain was too rough. We were completely connected and completely isolated at the same time. When Ann had finished the phone call, she looked at me with an expression so tired. It was better that the interview was cancelled. Describing our difficult situation to thousands of television viewers would not have made her feel much better. We didn't know which way to go. We had lost so much time in this mess. I suggested that we make camp there. Perhaps things would look better after some sleep.

We set up our tunnel tent on a ridge barely wider than the tent itself. Ann's flap opened to a deep crevasse. We had only four ice screws to secure the tent, so we searched for rocks the glacier had churned up and chunks of ice to weight it down so that it wouldn't be carried away by the wind (along with us inside it) if a strong storm should come. Ann gathered ice to melt for drinking water while I lit the stove to make dinner. We sat down to hot soup and a can of crushed potato chips apiece, followed by rehydrated fish stew and more chocolate. Tired and discouraged, we decided to call this place we had stumbled into "Hell."

That evening, we watched the high Antarctic sun dip slightly and the sky grow pink, a clear indication that winter was coming. The sun never sets during the summers, so the evening hour is a long flirtation between the sun and the horizon, like lovers who gaze at each other from across a room but never touch. Wisps of cloud turned violet and streaks of sapphire blue appeared behind the peaks of the white-capped mountains with giant glaciers suspended between them. Just beyond the black, rounded humps of the mountain called the Matador (for it looks like a bullfighter's cap) there was even a bit of red in the rocks. I would not have traded this sight of the Antarctic sky for a thousand Caribbean sunsets. For in Antarctica, there is nothing between you and the sky—no trees, no buildings, no poles, no electric lines. You can see for hundreds of kilometers along the horizon, where the sky meets the ice under your feet. It seems that the sky is not only above you, but also next to you and in front of you. You are walking into the sky as much as you are walking on the snow and ice.

Even the dangerous jagged crevasses around us reflected light and shadow in beautiful patterns. That is the paradox of this continent, so gorgeous and so dangerous at the same time. Ann looked at me, and I could tell she was thinking the same things. She smiled and said, "Who could've known that Hell would be so beautiful?"

chapter two

SISTER SOULS

LIV

When I think back to the first time I met Ann, I don't remember feeling that I was meeting a stranger. I don't remember any awkwardness or unease. Sometimes, I think that must be the truth of how it was. We are so much alike that getting to know her was like rediscovering an old friend, like slipping on a new coat that is so perfect for you it feels as if you had worn it a thousand times before. And yet I also think that my mind has tricked me a little. Ann has become so much a part of my life, so much a part of me, that I simply don't remember what it was like to not know her.

But this is the way I remember it. It was October 1998. The terminal in the Minneapolis airport was crowded with people hugging their hellos with other passengers arriving on my flight from Norway. I stepped to one side of the flow of bodies exiting customs and gazed across the crowd, wondering, which one is she? As more reunited friends and families left the gate area, I set down my briefcase (covered with stickers of penguins) and waited. And waited. As the crowd thinned, I took a seat and laughed to myself as I thought, "If we can't find each other at the airport, that doesn't bode well for our chances of navigating across Antarctica together, does it?"

Earlier that summer, when I returned from being a tour guide in Svalbard in the Arctic, Ann's letter was waiting for me. She had written to ask me to join her Antarctic expedition. Though I had known of Ann and her travels, I hadn't realized before she wrote me that we were both former teachers: I had taught literature and physical education for ten years; Ann had taught physical and special education for four years. The crossing would be a first for women, if we achieved it. More intriguing to me was her proposal that we build an online curriculum for kids, based on the trip, that would encourage them to pursue their own dreams. I had been trying to write a children's book with a similar theme for years. I love Antarctica, and the chance to return was tempting. But it was the notion of using the trip as a trigger to inspire people that got me on this plane.

"Liv?" The last person left in the customs exit area stepped forward and shyly extended her hand. Ann was short, 5'3" (1.65 m), and dressed in a loose grey suit. She looked skinny, and I remember thinking, "Is she strong enough for an expedition like this?" The next day when we went walking together, I would realize that, although small, she was a powerfully built athlete. She had hazel green eyes and straight, shoulder-length brown hair that she would later cut off for the expedition. I rose and gave her a firm handshake. Her grip was strong, but her quiet voice showed her nervousness. I immediately sensed her warmth and vitality. I nodded and replied, smiling, "You must be Ann."

I hadn't come with any expectations of what I thought she would be. I did have some idea of what I hoped she would *not* be: a publicity hound, or a chatter-box, or perhaps someone who was more in love with the idea of expeditions than the trips themselves. I had encountered all these types during my various searches for expedition partners over the years. Good expedition team members are hard to find. Some of the people I've traveled with over the years were more fond of talking to the cameras about our adventures than actually doing the work required by the trip. Others who seemed strong and resilient cracked from the pressure of harsh weather and isolation, leaving the remaining team members to wake them and dress them and strap their skis on for them every day. By then, I also knew myself well enough to know that I didn't want to spend a hundred days on the ice with someone who needed to talk, talk, talk all the time. For me, part of the appeal of the remote wilderness is the solitude, the ability to be with one's own thoughts. I had not met many Americans who enjoyed this kind of silence. But I am by no means a recluse. People often assume that, because I skied alone to the South Pole in 1994, I must hate people, or have awful social skills. They are surprised to find that I can do more than grunt when I show up to give speeches about my trips. The truth is, I skied to the South Pole alone simply because I couldn't find anyone to go with me. The men who were planning trips did not want a woman on their teams; and the female sport skiers I talked to were not interested in the extended camping and harsh weather of an Antarctic trip.

I knew Ann would have her own set of criteria for an expedition partner and that the next few days would be a test for both of us. We shared a vision of inspiring people to pursue their own dreams, as we had both done. What remained to be seen was whether we were meant to chase that vision together.

The hour-long drive to Ann's house passed quickly as we talked about our previous expeditions, our families, our teaching backgrounds. And I noticed right away that we could also be comfortably silent. Ann lives in a beautiful rustic house in Scandia, a rural area north of the Twin Cities, where she has easy access to hiking, kayaking, and skiing, three sports that I also love. As we turned onto the gravel road leading to her house, I remember thinking that I could be arriving at my own cabin in the outskirts of Oslo, the place felt so familiar.

Ann's dogs, Chica and Blue, a couple of Alaskan husky-Lab mixes, met us at the door with slobbery kisses and followed us as we entered the sunlit house. Ann introduced me to her partner, Pam, who, with her blonde hair and blue eyes, looked much more stereotypically Norwegian than I do, except for her height, which is about 5'1" (1.55 m). Ann told me during the drive that one of the reasons she had trouble picking me out of the crowd (we had seen pictures of each other only in full expedition gear, our features covered by parkas and hats and goggles) was that she had been looking for a tall blonde and I have short, dark hair. She finally guessed who I was when she saw the penguin stickers on my case. That, and I was also the last person to exit customs!

Ann had not mentioned to me before I met Pam that her partner was a woman. My first thought was that I had been silly to assume that her partner was a man just because I am married to one. That Pam was not a Sam *was* a surprise. But it was not an issue for me. It didn't occur to me to feel uncomfortable about sharing a tent with Ann any more than it concerned me to share a tent with a man when I attempted to summit Everest with a team of men in 1996. So when anyone asked me about it, I just made fun of the question by saying, "Well, I have nothing to worry about because Ann prefers blondes."

ANN

By the time Liv and I met, I was a nervous wreck. A lot was riding on finding a partner for this expedition, and I didn't have a back-up candidate. There simply aren't that many women in the world of polar exploring, period, let alone ones who'd be willing (or qualified) to attempt such a grueling expedition—more than 2,400 miles (3,862 km) of skiing and walking while pulling heavily loaded supply sleds in temperatures as cold as −35°F (−37.2°C). I had already committed to the expedition, my second attempt to cross Antarctica. My first had been in 1993, with three other women. We'd made it halfway and became the first all-woman expedition to reach the South Pole. The killer for me was that we didn't stop because we couldn't continue physically—we simply ran out of money. We couldn't cover the cost of insurance for the second leg of the trek, nor could we pay for an emergency evacuation flight should we need it—roughly $400,000. A couple of corporate sponsorships that I had thought would come through while we were on the ice had never materialized. So this time around, I was determined that money would not be the reason for failure. Brainstorming with some more business-minded friends, I had found an entrepreneur who then helped me recruit a team of five to fund and launch the expedition. We didn't yet have a name for the company, and we still had to find someone to travel with me; but we knew, somehow, that there was great potential with this gang.

I knew Liv had what it took to make the trip. She had already skied solo to the South Pole and had crossed Greenland with another woman. The question was this: Did she want to return to Antarctica? And, more to the point, would she want to do it with me?

I'm kind of a shy person, and it had been extremely difficult for me to write to a total stranger and tell her about my dream—not the one about crossing Antarctica. I knew she'd get that one. But the dream about using the expedition to touch kids' lives. I didn't just want to make history as the first two women to cross the continent; I wanted to do my bit to change the world, too. I kept imagining how crazy that must've sounded in my letter when Liv read it—that was our first communication. As I walked up to her at the airport, my shyness completely took over. She seemed tall to me, 5'10" (1.75 m) or so, with blue eyes and short, dark curly hair. I remember noting the angular plains of her cheeks and her graceful, lanky frame and thinking that she looked almost regal. I think I said something brilliant such as, "Uh, hello. Are you Liv?" I was really thinking, "Can I trust you?"

That night, after we'd eaten a wonderful dinner that Pam had cooked and dug into the Norwegian chocolate that Liv had brought, Liv went off to call her husband, Einar, in Oslo. I could hear her voice drifting in from the other room in Norwegian as Pam and I cleared the table. Of course, I had no idea what she was saying. She could've been telling him about what a complete nutcase I was and that she couldn't wait to get back to Norway. But somehow, I just knew she wasn't.

We spent the weekend going for long walks with the dogs along the dirt roads and trails near my house. We talked a lot about our teaching, our families, and, surprisingly, not a lot about Antarctica. We already knew we had that in common. We wanted to find out what else linked us together.

One of the stories I remember Liv telling me that weekend was about her first great literary disappointment. Like me, she began reading polar exploration literature when she was about twelve. She started with books on Roald Amundsen, the first man to reach the South Pole (and a fellow Norwegian), then the adventures of Ernest Shackleton, who tried to cross Antarctica. At the same time, she was seeking books about important women who had shaped history, such as Marie Curie. A shy and introverted girl, Liv immersed herself in books, living vicariously through the heroine's adventures. She noticed, even as a kid, that the kinds of activities she found the most interesting—exploring, outdoor sports—seemed to be the province of men. Compared with the Hardy Boys, Nancy Drew seemed tame and boring. So she started actively looking for stories about women who wanted to do the same things she wanted to do. Weren't there any adventurous women to read about?

At her school library, she stumbled across a book called *Amor on Skis.* Well, a *mor* in Norwegian is a mother, so Liv thought this book was going to chronicle the adventures of a mother who skied. Her own mother was quite an athlete. It wasn't until she was seventeen that Liv could beat her in a race on skis. But, unfortunately, the book's title was in French, as in *Love on Skis.* It turned out to be a drippy romance novel about girls falling for handsome guys who were skiers.

I had to laugh when Liv described how betrayed she felt by that book. I had so many similar experiences growing up; I felt that the things I wanted for my life were strangely out of sync with those of most of my friends, if not the whole world. I think we both felt a little bit freakish as kids. We wanted such untraditional things from life that we both had to be a little stubborn to become the people that we are today.

One of my first chances to channel my own stubbornness into something positive came when I was a high school junior. I had recently transferred from a private school to a public school and was disappointed to find that the school system had virtually no sports programs for girls. It was around the time when Title IX legislation was passed mandating that public universities had to fund men's and women's sports equally. I figured that it was also time for my high school to wake up and smell the coffee. Besides, I wanted to play sports when I got to college, and I knew I wouldn't be ready if I couldn't play for the next two years. So I rounded up other girls during our gym time and started teaching them how to play basketball. I was coach, captain, player, and sometimes referee. I bought T-shirts in our school colors, took them to my basement, and painted numbers on them with house paint so we'd have uniforms. Then I called around to local private schools and set up scrimmages with them. We regularly got thoroughly whipped. But we had ignited a passion that eventually drove the school board to approve funding for girls' track and field, basketball, and tennis later that year. Liv laughed when I told her about my homemade uniforms, but I could see that she understood what had driven me.

Apart from our mutual stubbornness and passion for expeditions, we discovered we shared a sense of there being a larger point to these trips than just making them. I told Liv about my trip to the North Pole with Will Steger's expedition in 1986: seven men, forty-nine male dogs, and me. As we got close to the Pole, maybe five days out, I had a chat with Paul Schurke, one of the co-leaders of the trip. We knew we were going to succeed at that point; we were so close that nothing was going to stop us. But we had this funny feeling, the two of us, and we were trying to figure out what this emptiness meant. It wasn't until I returned to the school where I had taught and saw how excited the kids and teachers were to have shared this adventure with me that I understood. The emptiness came from not having a full purpose beyond my own ambition. That's when I swore that if I ever did another expedition, I would figure out a way to bring the kids with me.

LIV

One of the questions people ask me most often about my trips to Antarctica is *why?* Why travel to a place that is so frozen, harsh, and barren? Why risk frostbite, injury, and even death to trace a line with your skis across a chunk of ice? I'll tell you— I can't explain it. Putting that feeling into words is impossible. I know that some of my desire comes from the inspiration I find in nature. Whether I am skiing through the forest near my cabin in Oslo or paddling through my country's fjords in a kayak, I find a splendor and a deep sense of connectedness that brings peace. I am not a religious person, but the feeling is similar to the one I have heard some religious people describe: It's a reverence that makes everything else make sense. When I am in the wilderness, I know why I am here, what life is about, who I am.

In some ways, asking me why I go to Antarctica is like asking a poet why she composes poems or a painter why he paints. I think human beings are all driven to create, to express certain aspects of ourselves in what we do. It just so happens that my talents are greatest in athletics, outdoor trekking, and mental stamina. For me, an expedition is a work of art expressed on a canvas of snow, air, and time. Finding that out was in many ways no different from the search that any other person experiences when looking for the particular career or pastime that he or she is meant for—whether that is to teach, raise children, lead a company, or play the piano. Once you find that thing that makes you feel like the truest version of yourself, it makes more sense to ask how you could *not* pursue that thing. In my view, the worst betrayal is that committed against yourself by ignoring the abilities you possess. Not heeding Antarctica's call would have meant that kind of betrayal for me.

Looking back at my childhood, I think I was destined to go to the South Pole. I first remember falling in love with the lore of polar exploration when I was twelve. My father, who is a builder, had to do some maintenance at Polhøgda, the home of Fridtjof Nansen, just outside Oslo. Nansen is a national hero in Norway, something akin to George Washington or John Adams in the United States. He was a famous polar explorer who in 1888 led the first expedition to cross Greenland and who later played a critical role in securing Norway's independence from Sweden. His house is now home to an environmental research foundation, and on that day when I visited it with my father, the caretaker let me into Nansen's attic office. I sat at his desk, still exactly as he had left it—littered with spectacles, notes, and papers. I used his pencils to draw a picture; and when I looked out of the windows,

I saw the same view of the countryside that he had seen so many years before. As I sat in that great man's chair, I felt awed and humbled. But I also felt a stirring of my own ambition. Perhaps I, too, would one day achieve something great of my own.

After that visit, I began to read about famous explorers, starting with the tale of Roald Amundsen's discovery of the South Pole. Then I moved on to books about Shackleton, Nansen, and others. Across the globe, Ann was reading those same books and falling in love with Antarctica as well. We both found the story of Shackleton's 1914 attempt to cross the continent particularly fascinating because he was more than just a brave explorer; he was also a great leader. Just one day's sail from the continent, his ship, *Endurance,* became trapped in pack ice. The twenty-eight-man crew was forced to camp on the ice when the ship, frozen fast for ten months, was crushed and destroyed by the ice. A few months later, the floes began to break up, so the men packed into the ship's scavenged lifeboats. After more than six miserable days at sea with little drinking water or food, the crew arrived at Elephant Island. From there, Shackleton launched what is now considered one of the greatest journeys in maritime history by sailing 800 miles (1,288 km) in some of the world's most turbulent seas to find help at South Georgia Island. After landing on the western shore of the island, Shackleton led a three-man party across the mountains of South Georgia—22 miles (35 km) across the interior of an island that had never been mapped— to reach a small whaling camp on the opposite side. Shackleton organized a rescue team and saved all the men he had left behind on Elephant Island. Although none of the men directly under Shackleton's command perished, the *Aurora,* which was to meet Shackleton's party at the Ross Ice Shelf after the successful crossing, lost three crew members. The *Aurora* suffered the same fate as the *Endurance* when it became trapped in pack ice at the opposite side of the continent in the Ross Sea.

I remember thinking as a young girl that Shackleton was heroic, not only for his incredible feat of survival, but for the grace and compassion with which he approached the task. He turned his crew into a community in which all men, whether officers or seamen, were treated equally. He organized dog races and sing-alongs in a makeshift pub to keep the crew's spirits up. And he never gave up—a legendary proof of mental and emotional mettle, given the odds he and his crew faced.

As Ann and I talked about Shackleton and other explorers, it was clear that both of us were fascinated by the way Antarctica had tested Shackleton, and what it brought out of him as a result. Even as children, we had both been enchanted with the idea of facing that same test, eager to see what it would bring out in us.

ANN

On Monday, I took Liv into our offices to meet the rest of the crew. It was typically chaotic with music, laughter, and shouting. We had rented a corner on the fourth floor of an old converted warehouse for the six of us. It was a loft space, so we'd thrown up a couple of walls and arranged the furniture so that we had something resembling "rooms." But almost everything was still in disarray. We had a hodge-podge of borrowed desks, a few squishy chairs. It was not an impressive office by any stretch. But it was ours. Already, we had a collection of penguins in all shapes and sizes—stuffed, inflatable, porcelain, plastic. The hallway by the bathroom had been designated as the dart board corridor, so you had to knock on your way *out* of the john to make sure you wouldn't lose an eye to a game in progress.

As I crossed the creaky wooden floors to introduce Liv, I felt the familiar jolt of shock and surprise: Why are all these people here? I still couldn't wrap my head around why this group had left safe corporate jobs to work on the crazy project of sending me across the continent of Antarctica. But I already knew that all of them were as committed to the dream as I was. And as a veteran expedition leader, I knew that this trek would entail a personal internal journey for each of them as well.

Charlie Hartwell, thirty-eight, our boyish-looking CEO, was the business brains of the group. He came with a Harvard MBA and years of executive experience in corporate America. He has a big heart as well. Shortly after he and his wife were married, they spent a year together in Kenya where they founded a nonprofit in the poor neighborhoods of Nairobi. An absent-minded dreamer, Charlie would be spouting brilliant marketing plans one minute and the next he'd be running around late for a meeting, shirttail untucked, black curly hair a mess, a coffee stain on his tie, bare feet shoved into his loafers. We loved his quirks as much as his smarts. That was just Charlie.

John Tuttle, thirty-two, our technology expert, is a Swiss Army knife of a guy. He's one of those people who can fix anything, whether it's a lawnmower or a computer. But there's more to him than that. He's also a geologist, a singer in a local folk band, a fifth-generation heir to the popular Midwestern Gedney Pickle Company, and a craftsman who builds guitars by hand. Shortly after he joined the team, John brought in an old guitar that he'd fixed to hang in the office. He'd replaced the pick guard with a new one shaped like Antarctica. That was the start of a collection of old instruments that started to show up around the office—a harmonica, a banjo, an antique violin. Impromptu jam sessions became a regular thing. And, for me, I guess it was the first sign of how this journey would bleed into other parts of my coworkers lives. I grew to know spouses and kids as well as the team members themselves, to the point where we all began to blur into one big family, related by our shared passion for this trip.

Then there was Anne Atwood, thirty-three. An energetic, freckled redhead, Atwood lives her life just a step and a half away from utter chaos. She is mother to three boys and manages to combine raising them with an intense career. It always seems that the more she has to do, the more energy she has. Atwood had spent years marketing for Rollerblade, so she came to us with an understanding of fringe sports. She was also excited to be working on a women's project after years of working with a sport dominated by teenage boys. I remember her telling me in her interview that if Charlie and I hired her, there was no way that this expedition would suffer the same fate as my previous women's expedition—lack of funds. Looking at the determined line of her mouth, I had no doubt that she was right.

Stan Oleson was the first hire that Charlie and I made. At first, I didn't understand why Charlie thought the first person we needed on board was a lawyer. It didn't make sense to me. Until I met Stan. Stan, forty-six, had spent his career in corporate law, but he was itching to do something more creative. He turned out to be a great jack-of-all-trades—drawing up contracts one minute, writing copy for the Web site the next, then debating business points with Charlie. He is nothing like the stereotype of the corporate lawyer; a fun-loving and jovial man, Stan has a great talent for puns and corny jokes as well as a deep spiritual streak. I think if he had to classify himself, he'd say he was a Buddhist, and his sensibility toward life was very much shaped by growing up a rebellious kid in the 1960s. Apart from a more creatively challenging job, Stan had found a home with us, a discovery that was to become very important to him in the months to come when he began a separate and lonely expedition of his own.

Kristi Russo, thirty-seven, was the perfect mother hen, pecking at all of us disorganized chicks to keep us on schedule and in line. When Kristi showed up for her first interview for the office manager and researcher position, she knew more about me than Charlie and Stan, who were supposedly grilling her. What's more, she handed over a copy of Charlie's draft business plan complete with bright red marks correcting grammar and spelling. Charlie knew right away that she was the right one to add to the team.

I think Liv was impressed and surprised to see that I had a real company with actual employees up and running. Those of us in the small expedition community are used to doing trips on a shoestring: You beg or borrow to get the equipment you need. We have to do everything ourselves. But this was going to be different, and it was a luxury to plan an expedition with a team of business professionals helping us.

After I introduced Liv to the crew, within minutes John had drawn her into a game of darts, Atwood was chatting her up about her stepdaughters, and Charlie was talking her ear off about plans for the company. She told me later that when she walked into the office she could feel the energy in the room, the excitement and drive these people were bringing to the endeavor. On the way out to lunch, Stan caught my eye and shot me a questioning look, his palms up as if to ask, "Well, is she in or not?"

I waited for Liv to turn her back to me and then pulled a face and shrugged. I had no idea.

LIV

I had no desire to return to Antarctica. I had already accomplished what I'd wanted to achieve there by proving my mettle as a skier in a solo expedition and fulfilling my life-long dream to ski to the South Pole. When I returned to Norway, the newspapers asked me whether I would go back for another expedition. I said no. My trip had gone so perfectly that a second go would be anticlimactic. And yet here I was considering it. The longer I stayed in Minneapolis, the more reasons I found to eat my words.

After my solo trip to the South Pole, I wrote a book in Norwegian, which was called *Nice Girls Don't Ski to the South Pole.* It was one of the hardest things I've ever done, writing that book. I am a very private person, and it was difficult for me to describe my personal feelings about making that trip. A very close friend had died just before I started the journey, and trying to tell the sorrow I had felt, and how it had affected my desire to make the trip at all, was very painful. I remember that one day when I was particularly frustrated, I told my press consultant, Wanda, that I was done. Just forget it. I didn't want to finish the book. She was furious with me. "Liv," she said, "do you know how many women have been waiting all their lives to read a book like this? You have to do it. You must." I didn't really believe her, but I didn't want to disappoint her. So somehow, I suffered through the rest of the writing. The response to the book in Norway was incredible. I kept getting letters from women who told me that reading about what I had accomplished when I was forty-one made them believe in new possibilities for themselves. Many of them said they had gone back to school. A couple of women even said they had initiated long overdue divorces! I began to see the powerful effect that my experiences were having on other people. And that connection was as important and profound to me as the trips themselves.

As I tried to figure out how to explore this effect more, I met with a class of teenagers at the high school where I taught literature for ten years. I told them about my experience and asked them how they thought I could share it with kids their age to have an impact. They all had different ideas, the most common one being that I should start with kids younger than them because it was "too late" by the time they were in high school, a thought that still amuses me. But I received a letter after that class from a boy who wrote to say, "Listening to you, I realized that I don't have to be a lawyer like my father."

That was the moment I knew what it was all for—the trips to Greenland and the South Pole, my years of teaching. It all came together. I had to find a way to use my experience to inspire kids about pursuing their passions. But how do you build a curriculum for that? I doubted that writing a book for teens would be useful because some of the kids who most needed that kind of encouragement weren't going to be enthusiastic readers. I had been stewing over that question for many months when I received Ann's letter.

I was immediately intrigued by her proposal, particularly the online aspect of it. I was even more taken with the idea when I met the woman behind it. One of the conversations we had during our walks made me understand the reason behind Ann's dedication to education. She told me that she had always wanted to be a teacher, that somehow she knew teaching was something she was meant to do. But that was a difficult path for Ann because she has dyslexia, a learning difference that made reading and writing a constant struggle. She said she had always felt stupid in school, slower than the other kids. Sports allowed her to achieve and to fit in. When she got to college, she tried to keep her dyslexia a secret because she was ashamed. None of her professors or friends knew how difficult it was for her to keep up in her classes. To get a teaching certificate, she had to earn certain grades for her last semester. She missed the mark the first time, and got permission to repeat her classes. Her advisor told her she should quit field hockey and her other sports and dedicate herself to her studies, not understanding that the very thing that kept Ann in school was sports. She failed a second time, and the school didn't want to give her a third chance. Since they didn't know about her dyslexia, they couldn't figure out why she couldn't make the grades, or why she didn't just take the degree (which she had earned) and forget the teaching—which would've been meaningless to Ann. She called her parents and told them that it didn't look as if she was going to be a teacher after all. Unbeknownst to her, her parents called Ann's high school tennis coach, who was also a guidance counselor. He knew several people at the university. He spoke to the head of the committee and said, "You don't know how tough this kid is. If you just give her another chance, she will keep trying until she gets it. Just give her a chance." And they did. The third time, she succeeded.

The way Ann explained it to me, life is made up of those pivotal moments when someone touches you, or intervenes on your behalf, and changes the course of your life. For her, being a teacher was about finding those moments in her students' lives when she could really make a difference. And that was the belief she brought to planning this expedition. She said to me, "I don't think I can change the world by doing this, but I feel we can change one or two kids or somebody along the way by sharing our story. I look at it as still being a teacher, but with a much bigger classroom."

That was the moment I decided for certain to join the team. In some ways, though, I had known what my decision would be after the first few hours I spent with Ann. I had called my husband, Einar, that night to tell him my first thoughts. I talked about Ann and her ideas. He said it sounded as if I had already made up my mind.

At the end of my week there, Stan hosted a party at his house for the whole company. John, who is quite a musician, and Stan, the prankster of the group, had written a song for the evening. It was a lot of fun. I knew that they were all waiting for my announcement. But I could tell from the celebratory atmosphere that they had already guessed what my answer would be. So, after dinner, I brought out a bottle of traditional Norwegian spirit, Aquavit (Water of Life). We toasted my decision to join. And I told them what I had said to Einar my first day there: I had found more than my next expedition; I had found my *søstersjel,* my sister soul.

chapter three

A PATH PAVED WITH
ICE AND MONEY

The trip to which Ann and Liv committed themselves that October day in 1998 is one of the most arduous land treks on the planet. By 1998, fewer than ten expeditions had successfully crossed the Antarctic continent during the entire history of recorded polar exploration— nearly three hundred years. The precise number is open to debate because of the long-running and impassioned argument in the expedition community about what constitutes a "real" crossing. Some tallies omit expeditions that have relied on motorized vehicles or dogs; others leave out crossings that were just shy of an "edge-to-edge" traverse, or expeditions that relied on caches of supplies dropped in advance on the ice.

This much is clear: Ernest Shackleton was the first to attempt a crossing in 1914 during his infamous *Endurance* quest, which ended in perhaps one of the most heroic failures of all time: a journey that stranded Shackleton and his crew for almost two years, but took not one life under his command. The first successful crossing would come more than forty years later when Sir Vivian Fuchs and Sir Edmund Hillary undertook the British Commonwealth Transantarctic Expedition in 1957 using snow-cats, large vehicles fitted with tank treads for snow travel. Will Steger, the co-leader on Ann's dog-sledding trek to the North Pole, also mounted a dog-sled crossing of the southern continent in 1990. But only three expeditions had successfully used ski-sailing—traveling on skis while harnessing the wind with a square or triangular sail—to achieve a crossing without help from dogs or machines: the joint trek of Reinhold Messner and Arved Fuchs (no relation to Vivian Fuchs) in 1990; the solo and unsupported trek of Børge Ousland in 1997; and the 1997–1998 trek of Belgians Alain Hubert and Dixie Dansercour. Using sails, a skier can achieve speeds of up to 30 miles per hour (48 kph). No successful crossing had ever involved women. In addition, the route that Ann and Liv had chosen had been traversed only once before by an expedition. Their route added roughly 700 miles (1,127 km) to the more traditional route, which crossed the continent at its narrowest span. If Ann and Liv completed their route, it would be the longest known ski-trek for women as well.

In fact, even American women scientists were not "allowed" in Antarctica until 1969. Before then, the National Science Foundation (NSF), which now coordinates most U.S. research in Antarctica, refused to permit women to take part in projects there. And the U.S. Navy had refused to transport women to the ice for any reason. Although a few wives of whaling captains and explorers had set foot in Antarctica (more than one hundred years after the first man had done so), the first woman to travel to Antarctica for her own work would not arrive until 1956, when Russian marine geologist Marie V. Klenova joined a Soviet oceanographic team mapping areas of the Antarctic coastline.

The arguments against the presence of women on the continent in the early 1900s had begun with predictions about the inability of "the weaker sex" to survive the harsh conditions in Antarctica. More modern objections included the assumption that women would destabilize the male culture of the continent with cat-fighting, nagging, and sexual promiscuity. As recently as the 1970s, the "lack of facilities" for women was enough reason for some countries to restrict or even forbid women's presence. That slow, uphill battle to prove that women could hold their own in Antarctica explains why, incredibly, Ann and Liv's attempted traverse in 2000/2001 was a first for women.

Ann and Liv's route would begin in Queen Maud Land, the Norwegian sector of the continent. Seven nations claim sections of Antarctica; the largest territories are claimed by Norway and Australia. Technically, the United States claims no territory on the continent, though it does manage several research stations, including the Amundsen–Scott South Pole Station. Since The Antarctic Treaty of 1959, all forty-four signing nations have agreed to use the continent for peaceful purposes only and to share scientific research. But with the exception of its twenty-nine research stations, the continent remains uninhabited—and for good reason. All told, close to 4,000 scientists, researchers, and support staff reside in Antarctica during the summer months of November to February, when the sun shines twenty-four hours a day. More solar radiation reaches the surface at the South Pole during the summer than is received at the Equator in an equivalent period. But during the Antarctic winter, the sun disappears completely for several months and average temperatures sink to −58° F (−50°C).

Antarctica is the coldest, windiest, highest (on average), and—despite the snow and ice on the ground—the driest continent as well. Its terrain is both spectacular and dangerous. One of the most widely held misconceptions about Antarctica is that it is a flat sheet of ice. Nothing could be further from the truth. The Transantarctic Mountains bisect the continent and much of the coastline is ringed by mountains. Because altitude varies between sea level and 16,732 feet (5,100 m), Ann and Liv would be traveling in high-altitude conditions for much of their journey. Most of the ice on the continent is sculpted by the wind into "sastrugi," waves of ice from three to five feet high, which lend the surface the appearance of a frozen, choppy ocean. About 11 percent of the continent's mass is constituted by vast ice shelves more than 650 feet (200 m) thick that extend from the continent's edges. The ice that covers the inland continent is more than 15,000 feet (4,572 m) thick in places: Imagine a canyon twice as deep at the Grand Canyon at its deepest point filled with ice until it appeared level. No wonder that Antarctica accounts for more than 70 percent of the world's fresh water.

Attempting to travel 20 mph (32 kph) on skis over such terrain (this speed is necessary to cover enough miles in the short summer season) clearly poses multiple threats. Hitting a ramp-like ice wave at high speed while ski-sailing could launch a skier and her sled into the air. In other areas, thin surface ice, melted by the sun, might cover crevasses hundreds of feet deep—just enough snow to obscure the chasm, but not enough to bear the weight of a skier or a supply sled.

The expedition would have a narrow window of less than one hundred days of the summer season. With a distance of more than 2,000 miles (3,219 km) to cover, Ann and Liv would need to harness the katabatic (gravity-driven) winds of the Antarctic to travel fast enough. Both of them were eager to try the athletic challenge of ski-sailing, a little-known sport practiced by devotees in the colder climes of Europe and the United States. The rectangular or triangular sail straps to a steering bar held at a level between the skier's waist and shoulders. That bar is linked to a waist and leg harness, similar to a climbing harness, so that the full weight of the skier isn't borne by the arms. But the sport still requires tremendous lower body and back strength as well as expertise on skis. Only by digging the edges of their skis into the snow, as well as manipulating the steering bar to angle the wind and thus drive them in the right direction, would Ann and Liv be able to turn. They hoped to average 30 miles (48 km) a day, a speed that would allow them to make the crossing within the summer season with a comfortable margin.

But spending a year to learn to ski-sail and training for the physical demands of the journey would by far be the easier part of preparation for the trek. It would be much more difficult to persuade corporate sponsors to pay up to tens of thousands for the privilege of swathing Ann and Liv's tent, jackets, and sails with logos. Charlie Hartwell and Anne Atwood were certain that the expedition would garner significant press coverage, and hence, great exposure for any company that signed on. But even with its appealing mix of idealism and potential marketing benefit, the expedition could not guarantee a flood of new customers in return for dollars. Investment would have to be justified on the vagaries of improved brand image rather than a hard dollar return.

A few weeks before Liv's visit, the team and their PR firm, Haberman and Associates, retreated for three days to Charlie's lakeside cabin where they discussed the future of the company and the journey. They crafted a mission statement, "Promoting the achievement of dreams," and named the company "yourexpedition" in honor of the people who, they hoped, would be inspired to take up their own journeys after watching Ann and her ski partner (hopefully Liv) make history with her Antarctic trip.

The return to Minneapolis signaled the beginning of the expedition *before* the expedition, the arduous task of breaking the way financially and logistically for the Antarctic trek. As with any physical journey, that path was strewn with obstacles and marked by celebrations: moments when the team doubted their abilities and others when they felt unstoppable.

For Stan Oleson, the Bohemian lawyer, a very personal journey began a few weeks after he met Liv. He'd been experiencing back pain for several months, which was nothing new for the 6'3" (1.9 m) Iowa native. But it kept getting worse. He awoke the Tuesday before Thanksgiving 1998 unable to control his legs and unable to walk on his own. He was admitted to the hospital, and later that afternoon listened as his doctor gave him the results of an MRI scan: He had a tumor the size of a small plum wrapped around a vertabrae in his middle back. A biopsy confirmed that it was cancer.

Even in the midst of the fear that followed the diagnosis, Stan kept his sense of humor. One of the first stories he shared with the team was the tale of his trip to the hospital that fateful Tuesday. His wife, Kate, had been unable to park the car near the entrance of the doctor's office; so she dropped Stan off at the door and helped him shuffle to a pillar outside, to which he clung while Kate parked the car. The two of them struggled to get through the doors, Stan leaning heavily on—almost being carried by—his 5'10" (1.75 m) wife. As they hobbled through the first set of automatic double doors, a man wearing a leg cast, carrying a cane, and resting his arm in a sling, was leaving the hospital. He took one look at the unsteady pair and asked Stan, "Can I help you, sir?" The absurdity of the injured man's offer of help brought home the humor of their predicament, and the two enjoyed a hearty laugh.

Ann's first reaction to Stan's news was not only concern but guilt. Stan had given up a job with generous benefits as a corporate lawyer with Pillsbury to come to *yourexpedition*. She couldn't imagine that he wasn't in some respect regretting that decision now that he was facing illness. But as the days passed and Stan entered radiation treatment, it became clear that he was exactly where he needed to be. The damage to his spinal cord from the cancer meant that he would have to learn how to walk again; for many weeks he came into the office using a walker, his stride about six inches. Recuperating among the kindness of the small, close-knit team was a relief for Stan. "I wouldn't have wanted to go through this while I was still at Pillsbury," he told Ann. "Here, I don't have to pretend or put a good face on it. It's like being with family."

Stan's illness drew the team closer and cast their mutual mission into a different light. His face-off with mortality simultaneously put their work into the proper perspective of "just a job" and yet added urgency to the importance of living out dreams. As Ann watched the team intuitively support Stan through his difficult moments, she was strengthened in her belief that something unique had drawn these people to her endeavor.

ANN

When I set out in 1989 to raise money for my first all-women's expedition in Antarctica, it took four years. And I still couldn't come up with all the money we needed. In meeting after meeting with potential corporate sponsors, I faced doubt and questions. No one thought that four women without dogs could survive in Antarctica. Several companies bluntly suggested that we put a man on our team before they would consider meeting with us. One CEO actually reached across a conference table, squeezed my biceps, and said he didn't think I looked strong enough to pull a sled across Antarctica. I was so dumbfounded I didn't know whether to laugh or challenge him to an arm-wrestling match! (Liv later told me she'd had a similar reaction when she tried to raise money for her South Pole solo trek. One executive had asked her—a woman who'd already skied across Greenland unsupported—"Have you ever hauled a sledge, *my dear?*")

Despite the lack of moneyed support, my expedition had a grassroots network of thousands of kids and teachers rooting for us. We financed most of the trip by selling T-shirts and posters. To date, my American Women's Expedition (AWE) to the South Pole is the only modern-day major expedition that I'm aware of to proceed without corporate sponsorship. I wound up with $450,000 of debt that took me about seven years to pay off, with the help of the other expedition members. Paying off my debt was like the expedition *after* the expedition. I stayed at it, and eventually everyone was paid. And I refused to start any new ventures before I had that debt paid off.

Part of what I came to understand after that first trip is the extent to which economics is a barrier for women to live out our potential, doing what we were meant to do in our work. I feel I was meant to make these expeditions. And I was stopped for seven years from making a second attempt to cross Antarctica—because I was mired in debt. While I was paying it off, I met women who faced other kinds of economic barriers and I began to see the relationship between attitudes and money. When I had encountered stupid misconceptions ("Women can't do that"; "You're too small"; "Women don't belong in Antarctica"), I had thought of them as just words. The naysayers could think or say whatever they wanted, I was going to do what I'd set out to do. But when I looked back, I saw that because the people with those attitudes controlled the money, it affected our ability even to have a chance at making the journey. I finally understood that the economic barrier was far greater than any of the other biases we had encountered—it had cost me that first crossing and then it had deferred my dream for seven more years. So what I was out for this time around was not just to come up with a better model for expedition funding but to get access to solid funding and break the way for women who would come after me. If I could persuade big companies to sponsor me, then the next woman who came along wouldn't be sitting in a conference room listening to some guy tell her, "Well, no other big corporation has ever taken a financial risk like this on a woman." That gave me the conviction to say, "There's got to be another way to raise this money, and I'm going to find it." Or find someone who will help me find it.

Charlie Hartwell was that someone. From the moment I met him and listened to him talk about his ideas for the business, I knew he would be the right person to hire. Actually, I had some sense of that before I even met him. As soon as he heard about my project and that there might be a role for him in it, my fax machine was just clogged with copies of his resume, his ideas, his recommendations. As Pam and I watched these rolls and rolls of paper accumulate on the floor of my home office, we thought, "Who *is* this guy?" His unbridled enthusiasm was hard to overlook. At the same time that Charlie came into the picture, I crossed paths with a young couple who had started their own public relations company, Fred and Sarah Haberman. Their insights into the potential media exposure for this trip and their organizational savvy were critical in devising what would ultimately be a whole new way to pull off an expedition. Along with Charlie, they persuaded me that we should found a for-profit company and hire a staff that would secure the corporate sponsorships we needed to get across the ice. Instead of approaching companies on bended knee, begging them to give us money out of pity or charity, we would position the expedition as a business opportunity for them. The Habermans and Charlie were sure that we could find companies that would "get it," and one of the best decisions I ever made was trusting them on that insight.

Even though I knew fundraising would be easier with a team of marketing experts working with me, I was still shocked by how different it was this time around. Atwood and Charlie seemed to know exactly how to get access to the right people. It seemed that where I would've spent three weeks working up the nerve to call a company's marketing department, they had scheduled a meeting with the right muckety-muck in no time flat. I was also somewhat surprised to find that my being a woman had become almost a nonissue. (Although I guess that, because Liv and I had already made it to the South Pole, the argument that it wasn't possible was already defeated.) So the discussion wasn't about whether Liv and I could make it across Antarctica, but what would be in it for a sponsor when we inevitably succeeded.

Charlie figured that to cover the costs of sending the two of us to the ice, supplies, gear, and food for the journey, we needed to raise about $1.5 million in sponsorships. That sounds like a lot until you consider that the South Pole journey Will Steger and Jean-Louis Etienne staged in 1990 came with a price tag of close to $11 million. (Liv's 1994 solo trip to the South Pole was the least expensive in history—$60,000). The way that Liv and I were planning to travel—simply, no dogs, one supply replenishment at the Pole—was relatively cheap. The exposure companies would get to potential customers was huge.

Not that there weren't still people who didn't "get it." There was the vice president of sponsorship of a major credit card company who said at the end of our team's presentation, "I just don't think we have an interest in this project. We don't have any customers in Antarctica." In a hilarious example of database marketing gone awry, that same company wound up sending us a preapproved credit card in the name of "Antarctic E. Bancroft." But somehow, the rejection was easier to take with a team working with me.

We made a trip to San Francisco in February 2000 to meet with several companies. Some of the meetings were those John Tuttle had set up with technology companies, so he was along with Charlie, Atwood, and me. We had a meeting downtown that went much longer than we thought it would; but it was promising, and we walked back to our car really jazzed. When we reached the lot, we realized it was closed.

Lights out. There was a little teeny sign the size of a business card on the attendant's booth that said, "This lot closes at 3:30 P.M. If you haven't picked up your car, you can get it tomorrow at 9:00 A.M." We were all standing there in shock. I was thinking, we have a meeting with Apple to get to tomorrow! How are we going to get there? We're stuck! More people started to show up at the lot in the same predicament we were in, and there was some talk of breaking into the attendant's booth and taking our keys. Meanwhile, Charlie, who was pretty much surgically attached to his cell phone during these trips, was already talking to his cousin, Janet, whom we were crashing with that night, to let her know we were going to be late. As I tried to figure a way out of the situation, my mind was reeling; then John said, "This is ridiculous. Let's just call AAA." I was just like, "What are you talking about? What can they do?" John dug in his rucksack and brought out his AAA card and pointed to a line on it that read "Key-cutting services available." John quickly reached over and snatched the phone out of Charlie's hand midsentence, said into it, "Janet, he'll call you back," and hung up.

So John called and AAA sent out a little van equipped with an entire locksmith operation inside. It took about twenty minutes, during which Charlie went across the street to the police station to find a quiet place to make more calls. We got a new set of keys and were on our way. I don't remember where we had dinner that night, but I remember a lot of laughter. John did a dead-on imitation of Charlie twiddling with his pen cap during the slide presentation, moving the cap from one finger to the next as he made each point. Atwood made fun of John for carrying a rucksack that she thought looked like a purse, and Charlie pretended to be aghast that John had hung up on his cousin. We toasted Kristi in absentia for the amazing research she'd done on each company we were visiting to prepare us for the meetings, and Stan for his work in putting together the PowerPoint presentation. I looked around the table that night and realized that I had come to trust these people as much as any expedition partner I'd ever had. I would trust Liv with my life when we were on the ice; I was trusting this crew with my dream. They were the ones who were carrying me through this part of the journey. And they were proving themselves to be as quick-thinking and flexible as any trek partners I'd ever had. Even though we didn't have a sponsor at that point, I had no doubt that this group of people was going to send Liv and me to the ice.

The breakthrough for the team came the very next day. The crew piled into their AAA-liberated car and drove from San Francisco to Cupertino, California, home base of Apple Computer. The company's educational division had already turned down the chance to support the expedition. But Atwood was certain that the trip would resonate with the company's marketing campaign of "Think Different."

The morning meeting, with Steve Wilhite, vice president of worldwide marketing communications for Apple, took an unusual turn. As Atwood and Charlie prepared to set up their computer slide presentation, Wilhite waved them off. "I don't want to hear the canned presentation," he said. He turned to

Ann Bancroft. "You talk. I want you to tell me why you're doing this."

So Ann told him about her love for the frozen continent, her connection to children through her teaching and exploration, her belief that kids, especially young girls, desperately need someone to tell them it is okay to risk, to take adventures, to aspire to something so unimaginable that no one but you can see it. Wilhite listened intently to Ann's impassioned speech, then smiled and said, "Let me read something to you." He went to his desk, rummaged around for a bit, and returned with a page from one of Apple's ad campaigns. He read it aloud: "Here's to the crazy ones," he began.

> The misfits, the rebels, the troublemakers. The round pegs in square holes. The ones who see things differently. . . . They invent. They imagine. They heal. They create. They push the human race forward. Maybe they have to be crazy. How else can you stare at an empty canvas and see a work of art? Or sit in silence and hear a song that's never been written? We make tools for these kinds of people. While some see them as the crazy ones, we see genius. Because the people who are crazy enough to think they can change the world are the ones who do.

Wilhite looked up from his paper at Ann. "That's who you are. One of the crazy ones. But the thing is, Apple doesn't do sponsorships. We don't put money behind something like this."

Hearing the promising beginning of Wilhite's response, only to have those hopes immediately dashed, was too much for Atwood. Her consummate professional demeanor cracked. She leaned forward and tears began to spill down her cheeks. Voice shaking, she said to Wilhite, "It takes more than genius and passion to create, to be the kind of rebel that you talk about. It takes investment. All the artists and scientists that your ad campaign refers to, all of them at one point needed someone to believe in them and *fund* their work. If people like you don't step forward, then people like Ann never get the *chance* to change the world. Don't you see that? She won't *get* to Antarctica if we can't persuade someone like you to help her."

Charlie, John, and Ann sat in shocked silence. They had all been known to choke up during these sponsorship meetings. Ann often teared up when she talked about the kids, and John had become emotional once or twice as well. Hell, they could hardly go ten minutes into a presentation before Charlie, the softie among them, was in awe-inspired tears. But never Atwood. Wilhite, clearly moved by Atwood's outburst, said he was positive that Apple would "support" the trip. Apple just wouldn't provide any money. Then he ended the meeting. Exhausted and uncertain just exactly what they'd been promised, the team piled into a plane to return to Minneapolis. That trip, one of the more grueling rounds of meetings the team endured, would later be referred to back at *yourexpedition* headquarters as "The Crying Tour."

A few weeks later, Apple clarified what Wilhite had meant: The company offered to donate all the computers and technical assistance that the expedition would need. It was not cash, but it was a critical piece of what the team needed to succeed; and, more important, the deal gave *yourexpedition* a powerful partner who lent credibility to their ensuing attempts to bring on other corporate sponsors. All told, Apple donated more than $150,000 in equipment and technical support to the journey. Those computers allowed Ann and Liv's faces and voices to connect with millions of children from the ice. Over two years, the *yourexpedition* crew embarked on multiple tours of both coasts, ultimately securing funding (or in-kind donation) from an elite group of sponsors, among them Motorola, Volvo, and Pfizer. Ann would not have to go into personal debt to complete this trek; Charlie and his team had knocked down the economic barrier.

For Atwood, finding sponsors for the expedition brought her one step closer to her dream of making a difference in the way people perceive women athletes. Early into her tenure at *yourexpedition*, she accompanied Ann to a conference on women in sports. One of the presenters addressed the difference in how the media treats male versus female professional athletes. The presenter's slides were a rude awakening for Atwood: photos of Michael Jordan playing basketball in his uniform, doing a slam dunk, sweating, and looking physical. Then a slide of Stephie Graff lying by the pool in a red dress in *Sports Illustrated*. The collegiate mens' sports teams playing ball and the women's sports teams standing by a Rolls Royce in slinky gowns. "It was just hideous," Atwood later told Ann:

To me, the discrepancy said a lot about how women's contributions to sport, and women themselves, are subtly devalued by society. Suddenly, I realized what an opportunity our company had to make a difference, not just in a small arena but on a global basis. We could be part of shifting the way women are viewed by the world. That went beyond providing role models for girls to *changing the way people think* about a woman's place in sport and in the world.

After I made that connection, there just wasn't any way I was going to take no for an answer the first time around from a potential sponsor. Or the second, third, or fourth, for that matter. For me, my work was no longer about sending two women I respected to the bottom of the world; it was about turning the world into a place in which my boys would grow up seeing women as equals. I couldn't imagine a more compelling job.

With corporate sponsors lined up, the obstacles Ann and Liv now faced would be the ones they preferred to battle— the forces of nature and the limits of their own physical skill.

LIV

There is nothing like deciding to cross Antarctica to make your neighbors think you are crazy. When I prepared for my solo trip many years ago, I trained by harnessing three car tires behind me and dragging them down gravel roads. It was the only exercise I could come up with that was close to what it would feel like to pull a heavy supply sled across the ice. Neighbors near our cabin in the forest just outside Oslo would walk past pretending not to see me because they thought I had gone mad. Of course, after I made my journey to the South Pole and wrote a book about it, *then* they understood that I was just crazy passionate, not crazy *crazy*. This time around, when I started pulling tires again, people would stop me to chat about *their* dreams. One middle-aged man talked to me for more than an hour about his dream to compete in world ballroom dancing competitions. He had followed the dancing competitions since he was a young boy, fantasizing about one day dancing the tango himself. But he had *never set foot* on a dance floor because he was too intimidated! I started to wonder after a while whether I should begin some kind of therapy practice because so many people were asking me for advice and sharing intimate details of their lives.

We started this kind of intensive physical training again (Ann in Scandia and me in Oslo) three months before the actual expedition began. Also, we both needed to spend six months putting on extra weight and building muscle to prepare for the trek. But for the most part, during the two years it took to raise the funds and plan the trip, we just needed to remain fit.

By far the most complex part of preparing for the trip was learning how to ski-sail. Ski-sailing is a difficult, inexact art. You must be responsive to the ground under your skis and the wind in the sky simultaneously. And somehow, while you are steering to avoid trenches or rocks, you must manage the sail delicately so that the dozens of connective lines—each about the width of a candle wick—do not tangle into a mass of spaghetti. Because the sport is practiced by only a few dozen people in the world, all the necessary equipment is custom made. I located a sail maker in Norway who would work with Ann and me to find the right shape and size for our sails. We would need a range of sail sizes for different wind conditions—larger ones for lighter winds, smaller ones for strong, stormy winds. Getting those sizes right and then choosing the proper sail for wind conditions was a process of trial and error; and because most of the sails we tested initially were designed for men, who are heavier than either of us, the task was made even more difficult. Ann and I took several training trips to Canada and Norway to prepare for the demands of the expedition, and each of us worked on ski-sailing alone as well.

During the Easter vacation of 1999, I retreated to our cabin with my husband, Einar. My youngest stepdaughter, Birgitte (who was twenty at the time) came with us. While Einar and Birgitte cross-country skied on their own, I went off to test a triangular sail.

About twenty minutes into my practice, I hit a rock hidden in the snow and flew face-forward onto the ground. The sail, still connected to my harness, continued to pull me across the ground as I struggled to grasp the "kill" line on the sail that would pull it down. But the line had snapped, and I couldn't reach what was left of it as it flapped in the air meters above me. It took me several minutes to wrestle my way to a stop, during which time the sail pulled me, ungracefully kicking and flailing, for almost a full kilometer. I was bruised and shaken, but not hurt too badly because of the wet snow. I have been skiing since I was three or four years old, and falling for me is unusual. I decided I had bruised myself enough for one day, and I packed up my sail.

A few minutes later, Einar and Birgitte came skiing along to find me. I was doing my best to look calm and collected as they approached, thinking I was glad they had not come a few moments earlier. But as they came closer, I saw the shocked looks on their faces and realized that the deep trench my body had left in the snow as I was dragged was ample evidence of my accident. We all knew that a fall like that on Antarctic ice could easily kill me. The three of us skied back to the cabin in silence. That night, Einar told me that for the first time since I had begun my polar traveling almost ten years before, he was afraid for me. I did not know what to tell him. I was afraid for me, too.

chapter four

"SEND RESCUE"

In the week or so after Ann and Liv were dropped onto the ice sheet by a chartered plane, life back in the Minneapolis office took on a comfortable rhythm. Each day, the two called in to John Tuttle at the office by satellite phone to share their progress. He recorded their messages and turned them into audio files for *yourexpedition.com*. By Thanksgiving weekend, the two women had traveled a little over 61 miles (98.17 km).

The online education program—the idea that had driven the two women to undertake their expedition in the first place—blossomed into an international success. The woman Ann and Charlie hired to oversee the curriculum, Zoë Alderfer Ryan, helped pull together an incredibly diverse curriculum and community of educators. Working with a consultant, *yourexpedition* developed a series of lessons designed to teach concepts about science, language arts, health, math, social studies, history, and geography, among other topics, to children in K–8 by using Ann and Liv's trip to Antarctica as a starting point. That curriculum could be downloaded from *yourexpedition.com* free of charge. Also available on the Web site was a curriculum that the company developed around the theme of "Dare to Dream." The lessons encouraged kids to articulate their own dreams and then map out a plan to accomplish them. Offline, Ann and Liv partnered with the Girl Scouts of the USA to create the Antarctic Expedition Patch Project, an award that scouts could earn by completing lessons and activities related to the expedition. And in a stroke of genius, Zoë had devised a "Go The Distance Challenge," in which classrooms of kids collectively tried to bike, run, walk, or skip the same mileage Ann and Liv would have to travel to complete their mission. She also began to feed the names of kids and schools to Ann and Liv so that the two women could respond to specific questions or comments that came in through the Web site. Delighted kids got a chance to hear Ann and Liv speak directly to them from the bottom of the world. All told, educators from forty-six countries took part in one or more of the programs, and more than 3 million kids followed Ann and Liv's journey across the ice. The educational aspect of the expedition had already succeeded beyond Ann and Liv's wildest dreams. The mood back at base camp was ecstatic. A late start from Cape Town, South Africa, due to poor weather and other complications, had the team a bit worried about the schedule. But they were certain that Ann and Liv could make up the lost time once the wind picked up.

On Friday, the day after Thanksgiving, Kristi Russo swung by the office to catch up on some paperwork. As she flipped on the lights in the darkened office, she saw the message indicator on her phone blinking insistently across the room. She sighed and fished a pen out of her purse on the way over to her desk. Sorting through the papers for a clean pad on which to write, she punched in her voicemail code, expecting to take a message from the copy machine repairman or another vendor. But the message waiting for her made her hands shake. It was from the company monitoring Ann and Liv's emergency beacon. The beacon was sending a distress signal. The voicemail message didn't say what the signal indicated, whether there had been an injury or a death, or whether a rescue plane was needed immediately. But Kristi knew it couldn't be good news. Trembling, she pulled the emergency phone list out of her files.

The first person she was able to reach was John Tuttle. She caught him on his cell phone while he was stuck in postholiday shopping traffic just outside the city. John's thoughts flew to the geographical charts he and Stan had downloaded from the Internet that week. Ann and Liv were in an area covered by crevasses. Maybe one of them had fallen through the ice. His mind raced through the possibilities. How long had the signal been transmitting? How much time would they have to organize a rescue before Ann or Liv froze to death? He told Kristi to get hold of the rest of the team; meanwhile, he would call the beacon monitoring station for more details. Any hope he'd had for mitigating news evaporated when he reached the station. Ann and Liv's beacon was sending a Code 15: "Send Rescue Immediately." The team had to send a plane to search for the two women as soon as possible. The difficulty, hazards, and expense of a rescue were legion. It would take several hours to mobilize a small propeller plane equipped with skis (instead of wheels) to take off for the rescue. Even when the plane was airborne, finding Ann and Liv would be a challenge. The beacon signal could narrow their location, but a spotter in the plane would actually have to see the two women to pinpoint their location, a feat that would be impossible if a ground blizzard obscured visibility. Even once they were spotted, the plane might not be able to land unless the area was sufficiently smooth or stable. And one or both of the women might be injured or unconscious, unable to help themselves or to stay warm. Ann and Liv wouldn't survive long unprotected in the Antarctic cold. A knot of worry formed in John's stomach.

He arrived at the office a half hour later to find Stan, CFO Carolee Lindsey, and Kristi nervously waiting. Stan was already on the phone to Adventure Network International (ANI), the company that had flown Ann and Liv in, to arrange a rescue plane. Carolee had her arm around Kristi; both of them were fighting back tears. Stan wrapped up his conversation with ANI and delivered more bad news. The weather was stormy at the base where the closest rescue plane was located.

ANI would not be able to get a plane off the runway for several hours. But the company head, Annie Kershaw, comforted Stan: Ann and Liv were experienced explorers; if there were even a chance for survival, Ann and Liv would find it.

ANN

It's hard to describe the elation I felt at being back in Antarctica. The continent is one of the most colorful, varied landscapes I've ever seen, and I've never understood why other explorers describe it as a desolate stretch of white. It still stuns me when people ask whether it was boring skiing day after day in the same scenery. Anything but. Every day, you're chasing an endless horizon that shifts as you travel uphill or down. Sometimes it's above your head, or at your midsection, or beneath your feet, but you never catch it. At times, you can see blue sky above you and yet there's a ground blizzard around your feet. The wind swirls particles of ice and snow, and when the sun catches them you see reds and turquoises and purples. Each day is remarkable in itself.

Shackleton once wrote that "no person who has not spent a period of his life in those 'stark and sullen solitudes that sentinel the Pole' will understand fully what trees and flowers, sun-flecked turf and running streams mean to the soul of a man." True enough, and especially apt coming from a man who had been trapped on the ice. But no person who *hasn't* been to Antarctica can fully appreciate the splendor of ice sculptures molded into the continent's floor by the fierce winds and the wonder of a cold, white sun that never sets. I do miss greenery and other kinds of nature when I'm there, which is one of the reasons that I glued a picture of our house and green yard into my journal for this trip. Yet to judge Antarctica by the familiar things it lacks denies everything that is unique and beautiful about it.

By the end of the first week, we were into an area of Sigyn Glacier that was riddled with crevasses. It was also a flatter, less slick surface, so we were able to use the skis instead of the crampons. Skis were safer because they distributed our weight more evenly across unstable snow, but they also provided less traction. Our skis were lined on the bottom with a soft, bristled synthetic fabric called "moleskin," which better helped them grip. But if one of our sleds crashed through weak snow into a deep hole, we knew it could drag us backward into the hole with it. We made our way carefully, picking around places where the snow looked rotten (partially melted and crystallized), and punched the ground with our ski poles to test before we trusted it with our weight. Accidents in which trekkers or scientists fall into crevasses are common and can be deadly. Both Liv and I had punched through crevasses up to our hips or thighs before. And, famously, on a 1993 Antarctic expedition led by Norwegian Monica Christensen in search of a tent that Roald Amundsen had left behind, Jostein Helgestad stepped through a crevasse and fell to his death. We couldn't be too careful. But after day 10, the third day in a row in territory riddled with many crevasses, both Liv and I were feeling more confident. After dinner that night, I snuggled down into my sleeping bag and slept deeply.

The crew huddled glumly around the speakerphone on Stan's desk, waiting to hear back from ANI. Kristi tried once more to reach Charlie, who was vacationing in Florida with his family. Everyone jumped when the phone rang on John's desk. John glanced up at the clock: 2:30 P.M. Minnesota time (8:30 P.M. on the ice)—the time Liv and Ann usually called in. He made a dash for the other end of the office to pick up the call, but just missed it. It went into voicemail. With shaking hands, John dialed up his voicemail and hurriedly entered his passcode, which was 13. Coincidentally, "3" was also the instruction for the voicemail system to delete a message. In his haste to get to the call, John's finger stuttered on that key, pressing it twice. "Message deleted," the prim automated voice of the operator informed him.

"No!"

Stan and the others were startled by John's shout from his office and even more shocked when they heard the crashing of books, CDs, and files as they went flying. John was livid. "I deleted the message accidentally! My God, I'm sure it was them!" He stopped throwing things long enough to breathe and stepped out of the office to face the group.

"Look," said Stan, "We don't know for sure it was them. Let's just figure out what our options are now. How about if I take our satellite phone outside and see if I can get a signal to call them?"

"Right," said John. "And I'll try to send them a text message and hope like hell that they still have the phone out."

Stan took the phone outside while John typed in a text message to Ann and Liv: "Signal 15—Send rescue. Confirm

ASAP!" They called Annie Kershaw again at ANI twenty minutes later; she said she was still getting the planes ready, and they should call if the team wanted to abort the rescue. After that, there was nothing to do but wait.

ANN

That morning it was Liv's turn to make breakfast, so I was the lucky one who was awakened by "tent service"—Liv bringing me a steaming mug of cocoa mixed with coffee. Both of us were feeling rested and relaxed. We had no idea that we were about to face one of the most terrifying days of our expedition.

After eating breakfast and melting enough ice for drinking water for the day, the two of us began packing the equipment and the tent. Sorting and packing gear took about an hour. As food bags emptied and trash bags filled, we had to pay careful attention to weight distribution on the two sleds. Liv's sled usually took the tent, which we managed to take down without removing the support poles. We taped them all (except the middle section) together so that the tent could be rolled up like a hot dog and strapped to the sled; that technique made for a quicker set-up and take-down job. My sled usually took the laptop and technical equipment, including a solar panel inside a black padded notebook cover. When we camped, I would strap the panel down and open wide on top of my sled so that it could soak up sunlight. John had rigged adapters that enabled one panel to power our satellite phone, the global positioning system (GPS) device, the laptop, and the

Motorola walkie-talkies we used to communicate during the day. (Although we tried never to let enough distance grow between us that we lost sight of one another, we were often many yards apart while sailing, and shouting into the Antarctic wind would've been futile.)

Most of the day was uneventful. The terrain was too rough to sail, so we continued to pull, slogging across a mere 7 or so miles (11 km) that day. We took our usual breaks for meals and snacks. Both of us were tired when we stopped pulling to make camp and cook dinner. Once we had the tent up, it was my turn to cook while Liv acted as the "human defroster," warming up our electronic equipment with her body heat so that it would work. While I started melting snow, Liv sat up in her sleeping bag with the laptop between her knees. She had the satellite phone down her shirt, the GPS inside her pants, and a battery or two tucked in her socks. She'd settled in to write in her journal and make calculations for the next day's travel. Inevitably, Liv would forget where she had stashed stuff to warm it, so she'd go outside, pull down her pants to pee, and the GPS or a battery would fall out. And, of course, I never tired of making the same joke to Liv when she was the human defroster: "Hey, is that a GPS in your pants, or are you just happy to see me?" The first time I made it, she did a double-take, like, *what* did you just say to me? And then she just cracked up. When the equipment had warmed, we called in with our daily message for the team. We got voicemail, so I droned on for a couple of minutes about the weather conditions, how we were already sick of oatmeal, and so forth. After the call, I tucked the phone back into my sleeping bag. Later,

Liv decided to call Einar to tell him we had made it through the heavily crevassed area. After she finished that call, she noticed that the phone had downloaded a text message during her connection to the satellite. She handed the phone to me to retrieve it. I plugged in the code, expecting a wind update or a simple greeting. But the message that flashed on the tiny screen read: "Signal 15—Send rescue. Confirm ASAP." What was going on? If the crew had sent a plane, there was no way it could be recalled. We'd be picked up on the ice and "rescued" before we even had a chance to hit trouble! I read the message to Liv while I dialed base camp. Without a word, Liv scrambled up and ran outside to grab the emergency beacon from the sled. We had no idea how long the message had been waiting for us. Odds were that a plane was already in the sky looking for us. What the hell had happened to the beacon?

John's phone rang only once before he picked it up.

"Hello?" I heard him say, breathlessly.

"Hey," I answered, my voice just as tense as his. "What's this text message about?"

"Ohmigod. Are you alright?"

"We're just peachy," I said. "What's going on?"

John explained about the emergency call from our beacon and the lost voicemail message. As he was explaining, Liv returned from fetching the beacon from the sled. I had never seen her move so fast. The beacon was set to a Code 1, "All's Well." Puzzled, she turned the beacon over for a full inspection. There we found the source of our confusion: A chunk of ice from the previous day's storm had wedged its way under the plastic guard for the "emergency" switch, which just has two positions, "on" and "off." The ice had tripped the alarm. And, as it turns out, once the emergency switch is activated, the beacon automatically emits a "15—Send Rescue," no matter where the dial is set.

I could hear the sighs of relief coming from thousands of miles away. And then Stan asked, "Hey, do you guys mind? I mean, can you stay on the line and talk to us for a little bit? Can we put you on speaker phone?"

That was when it first hit me that they had spent several hours believing Liv and I were hurt, afraid that something terrible had happened. We were fine. Confused and worried for a few moments, but safe. And lucky. We had stumbled across John's text message purely by accident. Normally, we turned the phone off after recording our daily log.

It took a few minutes for the team to absorb that we were safe. They really needed to talk to us, to be reassured. So we chatted for a while about the weather, the ground blizzard we'd trudged through that day, Liv's pulled thigh muscle— anything to let them hear the sound of our voices. Even though we knew they'd had a bad scare, I don't think we fully appreciated what they'd been through. I was skiing three days later when I remembered that John's voice had been trembling when he'd said, "I'm really glad you guys are okay."

⌒ ⌒ ⌒

As soon as the phone call ended, Liv and Ann got ready for bed—and John Tuttle changed his voicemail passcode. Shaken and drained, the team retreated to a downtown bar for a much-needed beer. They were all stunned by their amazing luck. If Ann and Liv hadn't had access to the satellite phone in the first place, the rescue would have proceeded. If Liv hadn't dug the phone out for a second call, the two explorers would not have discovered the message in time. And if the weather had been clear at ANI's base, a rescue plane would have been in the air by the time Ann and Liv responded to the message. The team contemplated the narrowly averted disaster for a sober moment, and then Stan raised his glass: "Well, I don't expect to have a chance to make this toast again, so here's to *bad* weather!"

chapter five

WAITING

ANN

Were it not for the satellite phone, that accidental distress signal would have been the end of the journey. The plane would have been in the air before we even realized the beacon was sending an alarm. Liv and I would've had to get on the rescue plane—or figure out how to pay $300,000 for the rescue attempt and still be able to cover the cost of the ship we had hired to take us off the continent at the end of the expedition. Even if we'd found a way to continue, the incident would've wrecked the mood of the whole trip. I cringe even today when I think about how I would have explained that mistake to our supporters. I could envision the merciless headlines: "First Women's Antarctic Crossing Suffers Costly False Alarm," "Botched Rescue Attempt Ends Expedition." We were under a fair amount of scrutiny as the first two women to attempt this journey. But our emotional devastation would've been harder to shoulder—like a family losing its home to a fire. Who could have known the wiring in the house was faulty, yet they spend years asking themselves, "What if?" The remainder of the journey would have been plagued by second-guessing and tainted with disappointment. So we were lucky to have intercepted the team's message when we did.

But beyond saving the trip, the satellite phone changed the very nature of the journey. On our previous polar adventures, both of us had used high frequency radios to maintain some contact with the outside world. These are bulky, bungling things that add weight to the sled and require a ton of time to set up. Raising the antennae high enough to get a signal past mountains and other geographical barriers was incredibly hard. The radio I used on my first South Pole expedition had a fourteen-foot wire antenna that branched into a "T." To raise it high enough to broadcast a signal, I rigged it so that the endpoints of the T were attached to my skis, which I would dig into the snow like posts. (I knew of another expedition that had tried to "fly" the antennae attached to one of their sails—they wound up losing a sail.) It took about twenty minutes to set everything up, and then you still might not be able to send out a signal. Often, communications from the Adventure Network International (ANI) base in Punta Arenas, Chile, where my sister, Carrie, was monitoring the radio waves, were crystal clear. But she couldn't hear a word I was saying. We couldn't afford to station a radio person in Antarctica at Patriot Hills with ANI, so we had no real way to get our messages to Carrie unless ANI felt like helping us out. Luckily, a sympathetic woman who was monitoring radio waves for another expedition wound up relaying for us so that we weren't at ANI's mercy. Further complicating things, you had assigned times for your check-ins because the air waves are shared. So you could be in the middle of an area with dangerous crevasses, or a few hours into a good sleep, and you'd have to stop and dig out the radio rig. More than just inconvenient, the process was a distraction from the focus and concentration you needed to give to the trip itself, to each step you took across the ice. And it continually made you worry about the stress that you might be causing loved ones if you weren't able to make a radio connection.

Liv's radio broke during her solo trek, so she just transmitted her position and status with the same type of Argos beacon we were using for expedition. Although some people might be scared to travel in such a dangerous place with such limited communication, Liv was *relieved* that her radio didn't work. It meant that she didn't have to fuss with the thing and she could have the whole trip to herself—the freedom to dwell in her own thoughts without intrusion from the outside world.

So Liv and I were both understandably apprehensive about the amount of modern technology we were taking on this trip: laptop, satellite phone, global positioning device, and walkie-talkies. It was all light and easy to use. But we hated to give up the isolation. It felt as if having all that gear somehow diminished the adventurous feel of the journey for us. As remote as we were in Antarctica, we were almost as connected to the rest of the world as we would've been working in the office in Minnesota. We would call reporters for media interviews, and—because the phone was so unbelievably clear—be asked to stay on hold for a few minutes, as if we were just calling from around the block. I don't think that I've ever had an experience as mind-bending as listening to the Muzak on hold while sitting in a tent in Antarctica! We were many weeks into the trek before we became accustomed to using the phone for calling loved ones, though the daily check-ins with the team became routine—as much a natural part of the trip as pitching the tent. Liv and Einar eventually talked once a week or so. I could never track Pam down that often because her work schedule was pretty erratic. Being in touch heightened the highs: We were able to share good news about progress and struggles with loved ones. But it also amplified the lows: There's nothing more depressing than having to recount a day of setbacks or little progress to someone else. You're struggling to stay on top of it and keep your morale going, and then you have to deal with their reactions, too.

But we knew that to accomplish what we wanted to as teachers on this expedition, sharing the continent with kids around the world, the technology tether was necessary. That ability to connect became magical. Each day, more and more kids were visiting the Web site and hearing our voices, joining us for this incredible journey. For me, the phone never lost its air of mystery and miracle. The thought of our voices heading up into space, bouncing off a satellite, and then beaming down to the other side of the globe filled me with wonder. We became the eyes and ears for millions of children, an opportunity both overwhelming and profound.

Now here's the crazy part: That we even *had* the phone was a fluke, made possible only by a situation that we initially thought was a disaster—our two-week delay in Cape Town. It was a perfect example of one of my core beliefs: Things turn out the way they do for a reason, and with every piece of bad news, there comes a chance for something good that you didn't expect. If you acknowledge that you can't control everything, if you stop resisting that truth and becoming frustrated by it, then you're more open to the opportunities that "disasters" can present.

Ann and Pam arrived in Cape Town on October 17, 2001, in the midst of a sultry Southern Hemisphere summer. With them came 720 pounds (328 kg) of gear and a team from *your-expedition* to coordinate logistics for the departure. Mariko Miyamoto, a former colleague of Atwood's from Rollerblade, also came along to be a personal road manager and media handler for Ann and Liv during what would turn out to be a nerve-wracking stay. Liv arrived the next day with Einar. *Your-expedition* had planned three days of celebrations and press events with its corporate sponsors to draw attention to the journey's start.

The group unpacked and took up residence for the first few days at the Cape Grace Hotel, a luxury hotel on the waterfront. That first night the whole crew stayed up late into the evening to toast Ann and Liv's imminent departure over South African wine and traditional Afrikaans delicacies, including John Tuttle's choice of tripe and trotters (cow stomach and pigs feet). He swore, amid much skepticism from the rest of the crew, that both were delicious.

Early on the third morning in Cape Town, Ann awoke to an insistent knock on her door. She stumbled out of bed and found Charlie Hartwell standing in the hallway, barefoot and unshaven, his face white with anger. Before she could speak, he blurted, "We don't have a plane. We might have to change our departure point to South America." A rush of adrenaline jerked Ann fully awake. That wasn't possible! How could they transport all their sponsors, team, and gear to South America in time for the departure date they'd set? Not to mention the journalists who had flown to Cape Town to write about them! As her mind raced through the options, she inwardly grimaced: This was their first serious obstacle and she and Liv were still thousands of miles from the ice.

The logistics of sending people and gear to Antarctica are frustratingly complex. ANI is the only private aviation company that operates on the frozen continent—the risks of landing on ice runways, unpredictable weather, as well as erratic demand, have historically discouraged any competition. Other planes that travel in and out are military planes, their seats typically open only to scientists, researchers, and base staff. So expeditioners like Liv and Ann must charter flights with ANI, which effectively has a monopoly. The price for a trip can vary wildly, but usually the cost of flying people and gear to the continent is well into the hundreds of thousands of dollars. The price is based on many factors, including the number of passengers on the plane, which continent the plane departs from and where it arrives in Antarctica, what kind of plane is available, how many trips are scheduled for a season, and how much fuel ANI has stashed at its bases. Because few of these variables are within the control of the expeditions themselves, some explorers see the price vacillation as capricious or even exploitative. And ANI's interest in using its planes, pilots, and crews in a cost-effective way often leads to late changes in departure points, even for world-class explorers with international reputations. That type of last-minute change wreaks havoc on an expedition's meticulous planning.

On the other hand, flying in and out of the least aviation-friendly environment on Earth is not an easy business. ANI's founder and director, Anne Kershaw, is often pressed to find pilots who have the skills to land on ice runways without the benefit of guidance from an aviation tower. And coping with a client base of explorers (who are rarely well-bankrolled), as well as the costly process of getting fuel into Antarctica (and removing the empty barrels), has driven the company into more than one profitless season. Kershaw runs the company as something of a personal crusade, not a savvy business investment. Her husband, Giles, a pilot, died in a plane crash in Antarctica in 1990. At the time, no private company offered rescue services or transportation to the continent, so expeditions that ran into trouble were dependent on the good graces (and resources) of the closest research or military base for rescue and recovery. An expedition could be out of contact for days, even weeks, before a search began. Kershaw hoped that expanding ANI's services might help prevent another tragedy like hers. But despite Kershaw's noble intentions, her business practices have led to suspicion and general mistrust in the expedition community. Ann and Liv were no exception.

Liv had gone several rounds with Kershaw over her final pick-up at the South Pole on her solo trek. In case Liv was delayed and missed the scheduled flight, Kershaw wanted her to charter her own plane rather than catch a ride on a flight that was already scheduled. The price difference was enormous. Liv couldn't afford a plane to herself. When Kershaw continued to press her, Liv threatened to cancel her trip altogether and send out a press release blaming ANI as the cause for the cancellation. Liv got the contract she wanted for the shared flight, but she felt bullied by the process. As it turned out, she made it to the Pole with plenty of time to catch the flight.

Ann's relationship with ANI had been even more tumultuous as a result of a calculated risk that Ann took as a leader on her previous Antarctic expedition. During Ann's American Women's Expedition, she arrived in Punta Arenas, Chile, without the full amount of money that she had agreed to pay ANI up front for transportation to Antarctica. The expedition had already been delayed a year for lack of funds, and Ann felt that if she postponed it again, the trip would never happen.

She was counting on a couple of promising corporate sponsorships coming through while the women were on the ice; when those didn't materialize, the expedition wound up in debt to ANI for more than $450,000 at the end of the journey, an amount that was eventually re-negotiated and paid off. Ann still looks back on that decision as the most regrettable event of her career in polar exploration.

Because of Ann's history with ANI, Stan Oleson, *yourexpedition*'s lawyer, and Liv handled most of the negotiations. The initial price quoted to take Ann, Liv, and their gear to the continent was $164,000, a price that depended on the presence of two other expeditions in the plane. Both those teams were unable to pull together enough money for the flight and bailed just days before the scheduled departure—once Ann and Liv were already in Cape Town. That left Ann and Liv the sole expedition wanting to depart from South Africa. Kershaw said if Ann and Liv were willing to relocate themselves and their gear to Punta Arenas, Chile (using commercial flights at their own expense), ANI's price was $350,000. Otherwise, if Ann and Liv wanted to stick with the Cape Town departure, the price would jump to $800,000.

Unfortunately, changing the departure location a few days before they had intended to land on the ice was far more than an inconvenience for Ann and Liv. Both feared that the amount of time to get the gear through customs would delay the trip too long. Flying out of Punta Arenas would also mean landing at a different base initially in Antarctica, one far from where Ann and Liv wanted to begin their trek. Flying to their starting point once they were on the continent could take weeks as well; small planes must fly out to deposit caches of fuel on the ice before a trip can be made. If the delay ate too far into the brief respite of summer weather, the two women would be unable to complete the trek that season. They would have to cancel the trip and wait for the *following* summer. For *your expedition*, the situation was a full-scale crisis.

After a hasty team meeting, the group decided to fight for a Cape Town departure. ANI's first offer of $800,000 infuriated Charlie. He decided to lobby ANI to reduce its price, but at the same time, to find an alternative: hire a military or freelance plane and pilot, which no other expedition had ever tried, in part because of the difficulty of finding pilots who can land on ice. The hotel conference room became a frenetic hub of activity, with Charlie's brother-in-law, Jeff Heegaard (a successful entrepreneur and friend of Ann's who had traveled to Cape Town to see the expedition off), calling every business or military connection he had to scrounge a plane and a pilot. Jeff gathered leads from a mix of U.S., Argentine, and South African military officers with control over planes close to Johannesburg. Charlie and the team used the Internet to track down the executive who headed the tourism company that had recently purchased ANI and was effectively Kershaw's new boss. Jeff called the man at home in Florida at 5:00 A.M. on a Saturday to make Ann and Liv's case and beg for a more reasonable price. "We're sitting here in South Africa with ninety or so business partners we've flown in, with hundreds of thousands of dollars invested in this expedition, completely at the mercy of your employee's whim on pricing a plane," Jeff told him. "And I expect you to do something about it." As it turned out, the executive was (like Jeff) originally from Minnesota, so the two wound up having a friendly conversation about their home state. The CEO said he would call back in a few hours and promised to do what he could in the meantime.

It's unclear whether the CEO contacted Kershaw, and, if he did, whether he said something that moved the discussion in a direction it wouldn't have gone anyway or without his input, but the end result was what *yourexpedition* was hoping for: ANI's price dropped to $630,000. One week stretched into two as the negotiating continued and bad weather in Antarctica delayed plane movement. *Yourexpedition* continued to pursue a back-up plane.

After the launch events with sponsors wrapped up, the group had moved from Cape Grace Hotel to the cozier Welgelegen Guest House, an inn farther uptown just off Kloof Street in the Tamboerskloof neighborhood. The guest house was nestled in a strip of several single-story row houses. Ann, Pam, Liv, and Einar shared a two-bedroom flat. The back patio became a place to lay out and inventory equipment; soon, the walled-in back yard, strewn with tents, sleeping bags, and skis, began to look like a strange mini camp site.

Meanwhile, John Tuttle was working on another problem entirely: finding a satellite phone for the expedition. One of the original reasons to pitch Motorola on sponsorship was the chance to get one of the company's coveted satellite phones. Motorola was an investor in the Iridium project, which created a network of satellites that could allow phone calls to and from areas that were previously unreachable through telecommunications, such as Antarctica. But Iridium went bankrupt shortly after Motorola agreed to sponsor the expedition. Most of the engineers were let go, the phones were deactivated, and Motorola was eager to wash its hands of the entire project. Motorola provided Talkabout™ radios for the trip, as well as cash, but *yourexpedition*'s contacts at Motorola had assured them that no working satellite phones existed. Besides, the satellite network supposedly had been shut down.

But John knew otherwise. During the negotiations with Motorola, he developed relationships with some of the "head geeks" inside Motorola who knew that the network, in fact, was still active. They told him that the U.S. military was still using the Motorola satellites and had at least thirty operational phones. All John had to do, his sources told him, would be to get a hold of one of the silicon chips—called a universal chip—that had the right security code embedded in it. Slide that chip into any of the demo phones that Ann and Liv had obtained before Iridium went under and the phone would be active.

John had spent frantic weeks back in Minnesota trying to locate one of the precious chips. As a last-ditch effort, he contacted a local congressman, Jim Ramstad, who agreed to write to the United States Army and the Pentagon to secure one of the chips. The day before John left for Africa, he received a call from a public relations representative from the army. They wanted to help.

Once the team landed in Africa, Charlie was nervous about telling the representatives from Motorola in Cape Town that Ann and Liv might have access to their phones after all. But news of John's inquiries had somehow made the rounds at Motorola. On the second night in Cape Town, during a celebratory cocktail party at the Cape Grace Hotel, one Motorola rep approached John, clearly agitated. The same guy had spent weeks telling John that the satellite system was no longer operational, that the phones wouldn't work.

"How much do you know about the Iridium system?" he asked.

"More than a little," John replied.

"John, I thought I knew everything about this system. But I think you know more than I do. Do you happen to know if the system still works?"

"It definitely does work," John said.

"Really?"

"Yeah, really."

The man blanched visibly. "If you got, through some fluke occurrence, some use of it, please don't tell me about it. I could lose my job."

"All right."

Motorola had been a great partner, and John had no intention of getting his friend in trouble. But he wasn't willing to give up yet, either. His perseverance paid off. The next day, John received word from Stan, back in Minneapolis: The army had pulled strings and the chips were on their way. The package arrived several days later in Cape Town; after wrangling with customs and paying more than $3,000 in import fees, the team had three universal chips *and* new satellite phones—when they needed only one. That one phone, however, would transform the expedition from a journey of two women in isolation into an adventure shared with millions of people.

For John, securing the satellite phone was more than a win for the expedition; it was also a personal victory. Although he would always have described himself as stubborn, this project had represented a leap of faith that he would previously have seen as unrealistic, even a waste of time. But over the last two years at *yourexpedition*, he had discovered in his colleagues (and in himself) a new level of tenacity and conviction. He had watched Atwood make her seventh call to a corporate sponsor who had initially turned her down; he had seen Stan painstakingly re-learn how to walk after his three weeks of radiation treatment; and he had heard Ann and Liv reduce a seemingly impossible frozen journey to a list of gear and a map. Somewhere along the way, John had found himself redrawing the line in his own life between the spheres of the impossible and the possible, gradually shifting more of the ideas in his head into the latter camp. "I guess I felt like for the first time I was working on something that was *worth* that degree of perseverance," he said. "There was no way I could watch Ann and Liv risk their lives for something they cared about so deeply, and then be the guy who couldn't come up with the phone."

ANN

I'm not even sure that John's securing the satellite phone registered with me at first; I was so stressed about whether we would get a plane and whether it would arrive in time to make the journey possible. Yet while part of me was just balled up inside with worry, another part was watching this group of people we'd pulled together, Charlie and the others, just respond with incredible energy and concentration to this crisis. I was humbled as I watched them. I felt sure that I could not have done what they were doing. Jeff, one of the friends who had persuaded me to start *yourexpedition* in the first place, was a human typhoon working the phones. He was calling complete strangers and asking for the phone numbers for top military personnel who were in charge of plane fleets. And he wasn't pushy or demanding; he just acted as if it was the most natural thing in the world, that of *course* they would give out a personal cell phone number to him. And by some miracle, they always did. He got hold of a three-star U.S. general who was out on a golf course and corralled him into discussing our need for a plane! It was magnificent to watch. His efforts were key because they kept us in the game with ANI, but seeing him go was also a huge mood booster for the team. He just dug in and didn't acknowledge for a second that we might *not* get a plane. He was cracking jokes and laughing, having the time of his life in this huge pressure cooker we were all in. We had essentially set up a War Room in the conference center at the Cape Grace Hotel. The place was strewn with phones, computers, boxes, some of Liv's and my equipment. Everybody was just buzzing, doing incredibly important stuff on this crazy deadline, whether they were helping in the search for a plane, calming sponsors, or preparing gear. I'd walk in and shut the door and there'd be this almost tangible stress in the room.

And then I'd have to go back out and put on a good face for my family and the sponsors so they wouldn't see how upset I was. Most of us were on the verge of tears because the situation was so tense. Meanwhile, Jeff was in there thriving on the chaos, absolutely loving it. He gave us that little bit of levity that kept us moving forward.

Charlie and the team debated about whether we ought to tell our sponsors that the expedition's departure might be delayed or relocated. On the one hand, we might be able to resolve the whole mess before anyone had to know about it; on the other, we might not. And they had all invested significant amounts of money and time into the project. Ultimately, we told them—both because we wanted to be up-front and honest and because early on in this gig, our sponsors had become more like extended family than business partners. Although our agreements with our sponsors were all about business (financial support in exchange for the notoriety they would receive as a brand supporting an expedition that was a first for women), our relationships with them went far beyond the contracts we had signed. At each company, one or two individuals had become champions for Liv and me, making our case to people in their respective companies who held the purse strings. None of them were blind to the marketing opportunity our trip represented. But, ultimately, they decided to sign with us because our journey also touched them as individuals, whether that was because we had made our platform about dreams or because they, too, were in love with Antarctica. Take Dr. Fredrik Bendiksen, the country manager of the Norwegian division of Pfizer pharmaceutical company:

Though worlds apart, as young girls we shared a singular, snowy dream. Ann with her brother Bill (in Minnesota, above) and Liv with a cousin Bengt (in Norway, below) head out for winter adventures.

Training for the journey took many forms. Pulling old tires for the feel of 250-pound sledges (below). Liv learning to untangle sail lines at −40 F at Great Slave Lake in Canada (left).

A matter of scale: Filling fuel bottles while the transport plane refuels for its return.

Queen Maud Land, Antarctica and the dream before us.

Ann pulling her sledge up the Sigyn Glacier and past Ulvetanna, "The Wolf's Tooth."

Trying to secure camp in a gale on the Sigyn Glacier.

The cold can make you feel a bit desperate. Liv waits for the blood to come back into her white fingertips.

*With wind, we could sail, and typically we did so in single file
(here using 15 meter sails with flaps). But more often we pulled, and pulled,
and pulled our sledges over the sastrugi (wind-carved snowdrifts).*

*In Antarctica, there's no need to hunt for good campsites. You just stop when you're
tired and make camp right where you are. And wherever that is,
you are always just a speck on the horizon.*

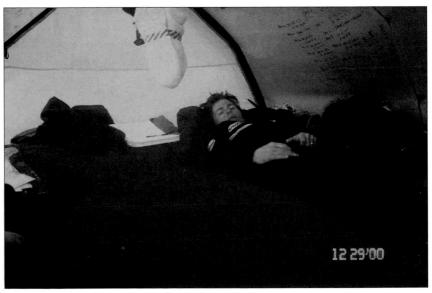

12 29'00

*After a 10 to 14 hour day, Ann lies still nursing her shoulder pain. Daily pen markings
on the tent reminded us of how far we'd come and how far we had yet to go.*

January 17, 2001. At the South Pole for the second time in each of our lives, we posed for a historic photo and then for a more meaningful one with the Tibetan flag and Dali Lama-blessed scarf.

Though being with others at the Pole was a bit overwhelming after so much solitude, the food was more than welcome (above).

Back at home in our tent Liv toasts having passed the Pole with Aquavit in fine Antarctic china—a film canister (left).

After one hasty meeting with Liv in a parking lot between conference calls, he had pitched sponsoring us to the global head of the company. As a former physician for the Norwegian Olympic ski team as well as for an Antarctic expedition in the late 1980s, Fredrik was no stranger to the power of dreams to drive people. He had seen how dreams had propelled people to endure great pain and sacrifice to reach seemingly impossible goals. And now as the head of Pfizer Norway, he recognized the need for dreams to inspire and drive a company as well.

Then there was Sören Johansson, the head of public relations for Volvo Cars of North America: He was a smart and savvy businessman, but underneath that, he was able to connect with ideas on a heart level. He was the type who greeted people with a big hug, which is not the usual protocol for typically reticent Swedes. After Volvo's charismatic CEO, Hans-Olov Olsson, had come up with a vision of why our expedition made sense for the company, Sören executed that vision with a passion. And as it turned out, Olsson's instinct was spot-on. Through their association with the expedition, the company wound up with one of the highest returns on investment they'd ever had from a sponsorship project. In short, our sponsors had become much more than financial supporters; they were friends and allies whose belief in us and the importance of what we were doing had made the trip possible.

When Charlie told Sören that our plane budget had skyrocketed, he came back with, "What can Volvo do financially?" I couldn't believe it. Volvo had already invested so much in us. It was an incredibly generous offer. And Charlie said, "You know, that's not why I told you, and I won't take any more money from you. I wanted to let you know because you're our major partner." That Sören didn't flip out and get angry, that his response was so supportive, was just further proof to us (as if we needed it) that we had made the right choices about which companies to bring on board to back us up.

Although I was stressed about the delay, I have to admit that I was glad to be stranded in a place that was a second home to me. I spent part of my childhood in Kenya, so I have always had strong emotional ties to Africa. It was a place that taught me how big the world was, how much more there was to see out there. Though I ultimately chose to explore the cold climes of both Poles, the seed of my adventurous and curious nature was nurtured by the hot plains of Africa.

My family moved to Kenya when I was ten years old through a program sponsored by the Presbyterian Church. I have vivid memories of my two years there: attending mud-hut churches with tin roofs in the rural areas; walking into the back yard of our house and seeing monkeys and antelope. My dad was a social worker, so we spent a lot of time in the squatter villages of Kenya. I'll never forget my first visit to the local church, where my father and the rest of the family were presented to the community. These people, who had so little, gave us welcoming gifts. They gave me, at the time just a grubby tomboy who hated wearing dresses to church, a live chicken—huge riches in a place where its eggs, and eventually its meat, could feed a whole family. I was just thrilled with my new pet. It was only much later that I understood the financial significance of what I had been given and how huge a sacrifice it was for the Kenyans.

I was at an age when I had no fear, so Africa became an exotic playground to me. I built a bamboo shack to play in that was a replica of an African home. I had a small stove and learned how to make my own charcoal. I would bury a stack of wood till it had moldered enough to burn for hours. I became good friends with our cook, whom I called M'zee, a term of respect for a male elder. He had been taught to cook for Westerners by the British couple who had lived in the house previously, and so was used to making meals such as steak and kidney pie. Yuck. I spent a fair amount of my ten-year-old energy trying to persuade M'zee to learn to make American hamburgers and potato salad.

While waiting for our departure, Liv and I made two visits to shanty townships in Cape Town. For me it was like walking backwards in time into my childhood. The first visit was a tour, one of those awful ones where you stay inside the bus and gawk. So I begged Mariko to find a real way for us to meet people in the townships. She arranged a second visit with a local as our guide. We were welcomed warmly at a church service, where there was singing and shouting that reminded me of that little church so long ago in Kenya. It was like a homecoming. But it was a sobering experience as well. The challenge of going off on a contrived quest in a frozen world paled next to the very real challenge these people faced in eking out an existence for themselves and their children. The sadness of that contrast did not escape me.

The stress of Cape Town was almost unbearable. For me, it was an uncomfortable vigil. Every day, we would wake thinking, "Today might be the day we can go." We carried mobile phones with us everywhere and we were always packed, ready to leave within an hour's notice. Mariko made sure that she knew where we were every moment of every day. As one week became two, I found I was sleeping poorly. I slipped into a kind of fog. I was too tense at night to rest well and too weary during the day to stay fully alert. I wasn't getting enough exercise, though I was hiking some. Each day that I spent in Cape Town I could feel myself losing muscle mass and moving further away from the peak physical condition I had been in when I arrived. I was too distracted to enjoy much of the stay, the wonderful exception being a drum class that Mariko organized. Something about beating on African drums for two hours was cathartic. We had Atwood to thank for that experience. She and Kristi had found a lively bar where African bands played at night. We went there a couple of times during that first week, and I was able to see all the team members dancing like fools. Atwood managed to nudge her way into the band one night and persuade them to let her play the drums. Mariko found out that the drummer gave lessons, and so we wound up in a class with twenty other people, learning to beat on our drums.

The other event that stands out in my mind was a visit that Ann and I made to an all-girls school in Cape Town. We talked to the girls about our trek and showed them on a map where we would start and finish. They asked lots of questions and were very excited about the significance of our trip for women. One little girl I remember in particular. After our presentation, Ann and I chatted for a bit with all the girls. This little girl cornered Ann, and I could see they were having an intense conversation. Her teacher, Liz Barrett, who was standing beside me, explained that this girl, like Ann, had a learning difference, and that she was struggling to gain self-confidence. I recognized the look on the girl's face, that of a person who is waking up, excited to be alive. I carried that image of her smile with me to the ice.

But as I look back on those weeks, I can see them only through a haze of stress. Most of all, I remember the heaviness of the waiting. It felt as though someone had tied weights to my arms and legs. I desperately wanted to trade that heavy burden of anxiety for the solid physical weight of my sled behind me on the ice.

I was furious with Annie Kershaw of ANI. I did not think that the price she was asking was fair. Integrity and honesty are valued very highly in Norwegian culture, and I could see no justifiable reason for her behavior. I also had concerns about the expedition itself. I had not been as close to the preparations as Ann because I had been in Norway. And I was a little bit nervous about how overwhelmed Ann and the rest of the team had been in the weeks leading up to Cape Town. So in addition to the list that *yourexpedition* had provided for equipment, I brought my own checklist, the one that I had made up for my solo trek to the South Pole, to make sure that I didn't venture onto the ice without something I needed.

Einar was worried as well. On the first day in Cape Town, Ann dropped off the sleeping bag that had been ordered for me. She said that she thought there had been a mistake in the order and that the bag might be the wrong size. Sure enough, there was a mistake, and it was not a long bag. It barely covered me to my shoulders. I was upset that we hadn't discovered this mistake sooner because it would've been easy for me to bring an extra bag from Norway. Now we would have to try to find a down sleeping bag in South Africa in the middle of the Southern Hemisphere summer! Einar looked at me after Ann had left and said, "What kind of circus is this?!" He was baffled by the energy going into the marketing part of the journey—the send-off parties and events with sponsors—yet this basic necessity wasn't covered. I knew that Ann and the rest of the team were very stressed. No one is perfect and these kinds of last-minute things do come up. But Einar was so upset that I brought him with me to go over my equipment. Piece by piece, we went through my lists and checked off each item until we were both satisfied that I had everything I needed. Back in Minneapolis, Stan ordered the right sleeping bag and had it shipped to Cape Town. Einar and I said a tearful good bye at the airport a few days later. At that point, we still did not have a plane, and Einar left not knowing whether our expedition would be cancelled and I would rejoin him in Norway in a few days.

The other adventure that our delay brought was a game of bureaucratic tag over my visa. The visa I had for South Africa lasted only until Einar left, which was supposed to have been when I, too, would leave for Antarctica. But I didn't realize that, and I had been in Cape Town an additional week before I realized that my visa permit had expired. Mariko had to extend her visa as well, so she knew where to direct me. The officials I spoke to were upset. I had to spend hours in line at three or four different government buildings to have things fixed. I remember several absurd discussions about how they did not want to extend my visa because South Africa did not have an extradition agreement with Antarctica. (Nor does any nation because there is no central government on the continent!) They finally agreed not to deport me when I agreed to pay a huge penalty fine. Mariko was a godsend during this time. She had two mobile phones—one to coordinate all the journalists who were going to be on the plane with us to record our departure, and one for the *yourexpedition* team. She was like a gunslinger in an old Western movie, but with phones instead of six-shooters. She could whip them out of her pockets, flip them open, and answer both in less time than it takes me just to *find* my own phone.

We finally got word on November 11 that ANI had a plane ready. They were just waiting for a window of good weather to fly the plane from Patriot Hills, a base near Berkner Island in Antarctica, to Cape Town. For two days we waited, completely on edge. Because of the twenty-four hours of daylight in Antarctica, ANI could call us to leave at any time of day or night. We had one false alarm when we were called to the runway, all our gear in tow, only to find that the plane had turned back because of a storm. Finally, on November 13— almost two weeks after the departure date we had agreed upon with ANI—the plane arrived. Ann and I went to the runway at 9:30 A.M. local time, along with all the reporters and photographers who would ride with us to document our departure. Our plane was an enormous Ilyushin 76, a big-bellied beast with gigantic engines. While the plane was on the runway, Ann and I changed from our shorts into our Gore-tex™ pants and heavy boots. You must be dressed for cold weather while in the plane in case it crashes. (You even have your sleeping bag handy so that you will have the best chance of surviving the cold.) The inside of the plane was open; all the wiring and the cargo hold were exposed. There were jump seats made of red mesh material for us to sit in. The deafening noise of the propellers began, and we started to move. I was not close enough to a window to see tearful Mariko waving, but in my mind I pictured her standing at the edge of the runway until we were just a spot in the sky.

The five-hour flight was very loud, despite our earplugs. Ann and I ate a little bit of lunch, but it was hard to talk much. On board with us was a Russian crew and a team from ANI that would be setting up operations at Blue One, the base where we were landing in Queen Maud Land, the Norwegian section of Antarctica. Another explorer from Slovakia named Stannie was also on board. He had intended to depart for Antarctica from Punta Arenas, but when we came up with the money for the plane, ANI forced him to move to Cape Town. Much of his food had spoiled while he waited in Punta. That, as it would turn out, was just the beginning of his troubles.

Most of the space in the plane was taken up by 55-gallon (208.2 L) drums of fuel. We would fly for five hours, land, and then the crew would spent eight hours refueling for the return trip, pumping the fuel in by hand and then re-loading the empty barrels back onto the plane. Carrying our own fuel was of course very dangerous. A crash landing would result in a huge explosion, which made me wonder why it mattered whether we had our sleeping bags out! But there was no other option because there is no fuel supply in Antarctica, and all refuse (such as the fuel barrels) must be transported out as well. For this reason, Mariko had chosen not to ride with us. She was afraid of landing on ice with all that fuel. I cannot say that I blamed her, especially when Ann and I noticed several of the Russians walking around next to the barrels of fuel while smoking!

As we approached Antarctica, Ann and I both cheated and got out of our seats to peer through the four small port-hole-sized windows. We could see the sweeping mountain ranges lining the Sigyn Glacier. To the east of the glacier were the Holthedal Mountains, and to the west was the beautiful Fenriskjeften range with its spectacular peak of Ulvetanna (the Wolf's Tooth). Looking at the stunning granite walls of the mountains as we flew over them, my thoughts wandered to my ancestors, who had given the mountains such a fierce name. According to Norse mythology, Fenris the wolf was the son of Loke, a god linked to malice and wickedness, and his wife, the giant Angerbodaj. Fenris grew swiftly into adolescence and became violent. To contain him, Odin, the king of the gods, ordered the wise dwarfs of the south to make a chain using the roots of the mountains, the sound of the cat's steps, the breath of the fish, the beard of a woman, and spittle from the birds. But Fenris the wolf managed to break free. He swallowed the sun and attacked the world with his jaw open between Earth and heaven. He also swallowed Odin, and the whole world sank into Ragnarokk, the "Twilight of the Gods." When Fenris was ultimately defeated, his jaw lay wide open, forming the mountains below us. It was a violent story to explain such beauty. The weather was perfect for landing: low winds and sunny. I held my breath as the plane touched down.

The ANI plane that Ann and Liv finally boarded in Cape Town wound up costing the expedition $500,000. But Charlie turned the exorbitant purchase into a strategic marketing opportunity. The team, including Fred and Sarah Haberman's PR firm, offered the empty seats free of charge to additional journalists, who thus ensured that compelling images of Ann and Liv setting off on their dream adventure would be broadcast around the world. Footage of the two of them trudging toward the white horizon with their sleds captured by the Associated Press would later be used by several morning shows and nightly news programs in stories about the expedition. To her credit, Kershaw had also referred several clients to *yourexpedition* to buy empty seats or cargo space on the plane. It was a repeated theme in Cape Town—turning disaster into opportunity. Without the delay, John would never have succeeded in getting the satellite phones. That quirk of fate meant that Ann and Liv would be able to do live interviews from Antarctica with the media, including what would develop into twice weekly discussions with Daryn Kagan of CNN. More important, the phone would deliver Ann and Liv's voices to millions of kids through *yourexpedition.com*.

Despite the logistical challenges they'd encountered in Africa, Charlie had no regrets about the decision to launch the expedition there. During the two-week delay, most of the *yourexpedition* team had returned to Minneapolis, John Tuttle and Mariko being the last to depart Cape Town. Charlie remained in South Africa to go on a safari with his family near Kruger National Park in the eastern part of South Africa. Being in Africa was a homecoming for Charlie as well. In 1986, he had cofounded a nonprofit there in the poor neighborhoods of Kenya shortly after graduating from college. The focus of the organization, Provide International, was offering basic health and social services to the community. After helping establish the organization, he helped nurture Provide from afar after he had returned to the United States; he returned two years later with his wife, Robin, to live and work in Kenya. In the year they spent there together, the couple focused on transitioning the leadership of the organization to the locals so that the vision and support of the community would shape its growth. More than ten years later, Provide International is a thriving nonprofit that has received international recognition over the years: The agency built the only hospital in Kenya's poorest neighborhoods that has a maternity ward, provided the only source of fresh water there during a cholera outbreak in the early 1990s, and sent one of only three ambulances that were able to respond when the U.S. embassy in Nairobi was blown up in a terrorist attack.

For Charlie, his return to Africa was a chance to revisit a place he cared deeply about and to share the country for the first time with his seven-year-old daughter, Lucy. He looked on Ann and Liv's time in Cape Town as an echo of the work he had done so long ago in Kenya. Like the seed he had planted, the dreams and inspiration that the two explorers had shared with the children in Cape Town would take root and grow on their own. "We knew going through Cape Town was a less-traveled way," he said. "We could've done it cheaper and easier through Chile. But our mission is all about affecting people's lives. There couldn't have been a more appropriate time in history or a better place to make a difference than in South Africa. Did we have a huge impact on the city? The whole city? Probably not. But many kids there will remember the expedition, and Ann and Liv, for the rest of their lives."

And for Charlie, Cape Town was a turning point. For the first time, he realized that in the midst of promoting Ann and Liv's dream, he was in fact, living out his own; for years he had hoped to find work that combined his head for business with his passion to make a difference in the world. He couldn't fathom wanting to make the trip that Ann and Liv had just begun. But if they loved waking up in Antarctica half as much as he loved waking up in Minneapolis as the CEO of *yourexpedition*, he knew the two women would not just endure the days ahead; they would revel in them.

chapter six

UNDERWAY, OVERWHELMED

LIV

Ann woke me at 7:30 on our first morning on the ice. I hadn't slept well. I was still jittery and apprehensive from the wait, like a runner poised in the starting blocks too long. My muscles tingled with pent-up nervous energy. It would be several days into our trek up the Sigyn Glacier before I slept well. Ann fired up the stove to melt ice for the coffee and cocoa mixture that was to become our staple pick-me-up in the morning. It took four hours every day (two hours each morning and two hours each evening) to melt enough ice for one day for the two of us. We would keep the water in insulated thermoses to prevent it from freezing again. We used that water to make all our hot drinks, as well as to prepare our food, 80 percent of which consisted of dehydrated meals.

My least favorite of the dried food was the dreaded oatmeal. Neither Ann nor I was particularly fond of oatmeal, especially when it was laced with cooking oil to add extra fat. It tasted like oat-flavored glue and left an oily residue in my mouth. But it was the most efficient way to make a dent in the high-calorie diet we had to consume each day to stay healthy. Each of us burned between 4,200 and 5,000 calories a day—more than twice the average amount—and if we didn't raise our food intake accordingly, our bodies would start to consume themselves, feeding on muscle to avoid starvation. Still, we would spend a few days hauling our sleds on the ice before we were hungry enough to stomach our full morning ration.

Our tent was a red tunnel of fabric with two small foyers, one at the tent opening and the other at the rear. It was about 3.5 feet (1.1 m) tall, so one could sit up inside but walk only hunched far over. We designated the rear foyer as our "kitchen"; this way, whoever was on cooking duty could have space to move about. While Ann sorted through our color-coded food bags for oatmeal packets, I slipped out of my sleeping bag and out of the tent. The view was just breathtaking, like nothing I had seen during my first trip to the continent. Queen Maud Land is rockier than my previous starting point had been. Everywhere I looked, I could see jagged black rocks and glinting white ice and snow. Hidden by that beauty was much danger as well: bottomless chasms in the ice that could swallow us and our sleds with one false step. The intense duality of this place was for me part of its lure.

When I met Ann, her plan then was to begin the crossing from Berkner Island, the most common starting point for trans-Antarctic expeditions. Berkner is at the narrowest span of the continent, where it seems as if the land had been cinched in by a belt, making for the shortest route across. But I had just read *In the Teeth of the Wind,* a book about two Belgians who had skied and sailed a trek that began in Queen Maud Land. I was fascinated by this route, partly because it was relatively unexplored, and partly because of the challenge it presented as the farthest region from our destination point. Starting there would make our route one of the longest ever attempted. And because Ann and I represented the United States and Norway, I thought it would be fun to start from the Norwegian sector of Antarctica, go through the Amundsen-Scott Base at the South Pole (an American research station) to the final point of McMurdo, another American scientific station. I was happy that Ann was intrigued enough by the same points to agree on the different starting location.

I looked south toward Sigyn Glacier. I wished we had time to detour and touch the mountains on either side of the glacier. It was more than tempting. But we were already behind schedule, so we would merely pass between them. By Antarctic standards, the weather was balmy: 10°F (−12°C). I was comfortable standing outside in my long woolen underwear. I couldn't believe we were finally here. The waiting weeks in Cape Town had been frustrating for Einar as well as for me. I could hear the relief in his voice in the last phone call from Cape Town. He loves skiing as much as I do and I hoped for his sake that the winter would come early in Norway. I knew that on the trek ahead, when I would be putting all my weight and strength into pulling my sled through the sticky snow, I would catch myself wishing I were at home and gliding behind Einar through the forest with light cross-country equipment and in perfect ski tracks.

"Haaaloh!"

I was pulled from my reverie by Stannie, the Slovakian whose food who had spoiled while he waited for transport in Punta Arenas and had shared the plane with us. He was attempting to travel across the continent by himself and had camped about sixty feet or so from us for the first night. He was a small skinny man, and though he spoke little English, Ann and I had exchanged friendly gestures and smiles with him. He was very sweet, and we were intrigued by his equipment, which was so different from ours. He had constructed a strange contraption to get him across the ice, a sort of tractor seat on shocks that was lashed to skis and harnessed to a sail. His idea was to sit down while the wind pulled him along. Ann and I were a little skeptical. That sitting position would give him no ability to shift his weight, steer properly, or react quickly if he fell into a crevasse. The idea would've worked on a flat, frozen sea, but for this rough terrain it was very optimistic—like trying to ski across Antarctica in a La-Z-Boy recliner. But what he lacked in experience he more than made up for in enthusiasm and childlike wonder. Watching him stand outside his tent and wave both arms above his head, I had to smile. He made a little jump in the air and swept his arms out as if to hug the entire horizon to his chest.

"Beauuuuteeful!" he shouted.

I laughed back at him with an exaggerated nod. Yes, indeed. It was beautiful. But I would have many weeks to savor its beauty, and my stomach growled insistently. I crawled back inside the tent for my breakfast.

Stannie was not our only company as we began our trip that morning. During those first few days we saw several white snow petrels that circled and dove, investigating the bright red dots of our parkas against the white snow. I thought we might have looked like flowers to them from the sky. When we had our blue sails up, they flirted and danced with the billowing material, almost touching the sails. Not having seen many humans, the birds were bold and curious, but we weren't very far along before they, too, disappeared. Although penguin colonies and seals are plentiful along Antarctica's peninsula, there is no wildlife of any kind in the interior of the continent. The conditions are too harsh for survival and there are simply no food sources. (Polar bears, which inhabit the *North* Pole, feed on the marine life under the ice, which spans ocean and not land, as it does in Antarctica.) Stannie, on the other hand, did not disappear for a while.

On the first day, we gave him a head start and watched him tow his sled, the heavy seat hitched behind it until he could find some wind, as he zig-zagged off toward the mountains. We set off a little farther behind, pulling our sleds at full weight, 250 pounds (113 kg) each. At first, the terrain was slippery enough with its rippled blue ice that we used crampons for better traction. It was slow going; we pulled for six or seven hours straight and traveled little more than 7 or 8 miles (11.26 km). We stopped every couple of hours for a hot sports drink (which tastes like a sweet, fruity tea) or water to stay hydrated. Stannie drifted in and out of our sight for several days.

Distance is a strange thing in Antarctica because one can see for hundreds of kilometers. I felt tiny against the unending stretch of ice yet objects on the horizon seemed so much larger and closer than they are because no buildings, no trees, and no hills block the view. So Stannie was a speck that loomed and receded in our view, but seldom disappeared. A few times we were within speaking distance, so Ann and I stopped to eat and let him gain some ground. There was nothing offensive about Stannie himself, but we were drawn to this vast, open place in part because we found isolation appealing. I, in particular, was eager to lose our Slovakian shadow.

I finally began to relax on our fourth night, when it seemed we had lost him. But when we were inside our tent eating dinner, we heard a familiar "Haaaloh!" I nearly choked on my soup, and Ann literally fell over laughing, capsized on her sleeping bag with her hand clamped over her mouth to smother the sound. Of course, when we had regained our composure, we offered to share our dinner with him.

That night, he camped but a few meters from our tent. I couldn't believe it! Here we were, with an entire continent of empty space in which he could pitch his tent, and he plopped down right next to us! I think that our presence made him feel safer, and I was sympathetic to that. Not everyone enjoys solitude as much as I do. And there was something very Norwegian about my discomfort. In Norway, when we camp after a day of hiking or skiing, it is considered rude to put yourself so close to another tent that its occupants can hear you. We have a country with few people and a lot of space, so we are somewhat spoiled. I was chagrined by the irony of feeling crowded on a virtually uninhabited continent. And Ann found my annoyance most amusing.

After that, we didn't see Stannie again, though we half-expected to. We later found out that he had given up and called for a plane pick-up just a few days after we last saw him. But for the rest of the trip, whenever Ann and I wanted to make each other laugh, we would just sneak up from behind and shout, "Haaaloh!"

On November 19, Einar's birthday, we awoke to find the sky awash in pastels, as if we were walking and sailing into a water color painting. The stunning display healed the frustration of having little wind and long days of pulling so far.

One of the reminders of home that I had brought with me was an envelope with messages from Einar. He had written these out in advance, about one for each day, so that the two of us could stay connected while I was on the ice. I would begin each day by drawing a random message from the envelope and reading it. Sometimes they were little jokes from Einar, or just words of encouragement. I always tried to think about his messages throughout the day. I drew a slip of paper out of the envelope. It read, "Cohen, and rødvin og m i Gjønnesskogen," "Cohen and red wine, and M&M in Gjønnesskogen." I'm a big fan of the Canadian singer Leonard Cohen, and of good red wine as well. The place he referred to is where I lived when Einar and I started dating. The gist of his note was that he had named some of the changes I had brought into his life, and indicated that he was happy about how his life had turned out with me in it. I think it's fair to say that I introduced Einar to a very different way of living.

When I first met Einar, he had a degree in economics and was running his family's wholesale company in the foundry trade. Shortly after that, I began to plan my first expedition across Greenland. Other men I had dated thought I was crazy to want to make these kinds of trips. I was thirty-two at the time, and many of the friends and family around me were beginning to wonder when I would "settle down" and get married. And in Norway (as in much of the rest of the world), that kind of expedition was seen as the province of men. My previous boyfriend had been indifferent to my plan to ski across Greenland. But Einar was nothing but supportive from the first day I told him about my dream to ski to the South Pole. The Greenland expedition in 1992 was the beginning of the fulfillment of that dream. We had so many conversations about dreams while I was planning that trip. He told me, "What I admire in you, Liv, is that you realize your dreams and plans." I had responded, "What is preventing you from doing the same?" He had always wanted to have a career in medicine, but had opted for business because of his family. So at the age of forty-five, he quit his company and went back to school to train as a physical therapist. Four years later, in 1996, he started his own physical therapy practice. I was thrilled for him, and for us—that we had built a relationship that encouraged and supported each other in taking risks. Reading his note, and knowing all that it referred to, filled me with a sense of peace. It is a rare and wonderful thing to have a partnership in which you are loved not only for who you are but for whatever you may decide to become.

Because it was Einar's birthday, I cheated and took out a second note. It read, *"Generøsitet=Liven,"* "Generosity=Liv" (me). That brought a tear to my eye, because I think of *him* as one of the most generous people I have ever known.

ANN

My first day on the ice, I awoke to the thrilling contradictions of Antarctica: Simultaneously, my world seemed to have shrunk to the size of my sled, and yet expanded to the edges of the horizon. Life was reduced to its most elemental: staying warm, setting up shelter, eating, sleeping. These activities were the constant undercurrents running beneath the flow that was the daily task of gaining miles, and I embraced that simplicity with eagerness. With each step tugging against the solid weight of my sled, I felt myself releasing the stress and irritants of daily life into the void of Antarctica's whiteness: no bill-paying, no cars honking, no meetings, no scrubbing the bath-tub, no television news of war or conflict, no waiting in line at the bank, no to-do list three pages long. Just a silence so profound that I could hear the blood rushing in my veins, a compass direction to chase, a landscape so beautifully empty that I could fill it with all my secret thoughts and dreams. The freedom of this kind of uncomplicated existence was intoxicating. But as the scale of life's concerns shrank, the meaning of things expanded. Little things that I took for granted in the "real" world took on a whole new importance. It's hard to explain the comfort I found in a warm cup of coffee after spending twenty minutes trying to detangle a sail line with stiff, cold fingers. Or the gratefulness I would feel toward Liv when she helped me sew up tears in one of my sails: I knew that generous gesture came from someone who was at least as tired and wracked with cold and pain as I was. Being in Antarctica, for me, brought an altered state of awareness—of my body, of nature, of our connectedness to something larger than ourselves. I was a tiny speck on the ice, but at the same time I was conscious of being tied to all the explorers who had come before me, of becoming part of the history of the landscape, joined with the continent in my struggle to cross it.

Of course, that was one way to look at it. Most "normal" people would see it as a ninety-some-day trip without a shower, a change of clothes, or a crumb of fresh food to eat! It's hard to explain to most people, but those aspects of the journey simply didn't bother us. For us, weeks of eating rehydrated fish meal, the physical aches and pains, the cold, the "less-than-fresh" feeling, was all part of the game. No big deal.

Eating on an expedition is more about calories than taste, anyway. You have to consume a high-fat, high-calorie diet to make sure that you don't lose too much weight. Most male-led expedition teams meet that requirement by eating sticks of butter. Liv and I, however, decided to add cooking oil to our morning oatmeal and down big portions of chocolate as a tastier solution to the fat challenge. Salt is another big diet requirement because we would lose so much of it through sweating. So we both ate a whole can of crushed potato chips apiece at dinner. The rest of the day's menu included instant soup, sports drink, pasta Bolognese or fish (rehydrated with water), and hot drinks. With that kind of limited selection, you find yourself really looking forward to the "treats." Liv's mom had made her special Kentucky fruit cake for us to take along, so we saved slices of that for days when we wanted to celebrate hitting a milestone or we needed a pick-me-up. On a few occasions, we toasted the end of the day with a shot of Aquavit or my favorite Scotch, downed from an empty film canister.

Small comforts became huge. My favorite part of the day was getting into the tent and putting on a dry pair of socks. Sheer heaven. And brushing my teeth felt almost as refreshing as a long, hot shower. Even better, when I had finished drinking my hot mint tea at night, I would take the tea bag and rub it on my face for a warm, minty Antarctic-style spa treatment! Of course, showering and bathing would be impossible until we made it midway, to the South Pole station. In the meantime, Liv and I carried wipes for quick weekly rub-downs. Not that the wipes got you entirely *clean*. But they would prevent skin sores from bacteria—a condition other explorers have encountered, though neither Liv nor I have experienced it. It might sound strange, but going that long without a shower is not a big deal. For one thing, you're in a place where it's so cold and pristine that you don't smell. For another, there's no dirt anywhere, so you're not covered with grime. And, as Pam says, Liv and I are just "gross."

As you might imagine, some of the fairly simple facts of life became a bit more complicated in Antarctica. I think the most common question people asked me after my first trip to Antarctica was, "How did you go to the bathroom?" To which I usually replied, "As fast as humanly possible." We would duck outside at least a few feet from the entrance and choose a direction that ensured the tent wouldn't be downwind from where we were making a deposit, pull down the snow pants, squat, and do our business very quickly. (Not bothering to look for a rock or tree to squat behind, since there are none. But there also aren't any people to spy on you.) Because Antarctica has strict environmental guidelines, you're not allowed to leave trash behind. That includes soiled toilet paper and used tampons, so you have to bundle that stuff up in a plastic bag and take it with you. Although I can think of more pleasant experiences than trying to pee, change a tampon, and wipe off without falling over or making a mess of myself, it's not that bad once you get used to it. I prefer it to using a port-a-potty any day. The surprising part? It's not your bum that gets cold during that whole process. It's your fingers!

When you have to drag everything you decide to bring with you in a sled, you deliberate long and hard about what you "need" to bring. Our sleds became our universe. The bulk of our weight, and by far most important item, was fuel. We carried white gas, a fuel that burns well at high altitude, for our stove. When we started the trek, we had about 7.9 gallons (30 liters) of the stuff. For clothing, we each had three pairs of socks and one change of long underwear. Over the long underwear we wore our parkas and Gore-tex™ pants. If we were ski-sailing, we added down pants and vests over the outer layer. But if we were pulling, our body heat was usually enough to keep us warm. Technically, a down layer would be more efficient *under* a windproof outer coat. But if we needed to add layers, stripping down to the fleece to get the down under the parkas wasted too much body heat. So we just put them on top. We each had two hats (one wool and one fleece with a Windstopper™ layer of nylon), two pairs of woolen mittens, and outer mitts that were windproof for sailing. I carried my "lucky" green wool hat that has been to both the North and the South Pole with me. Because of the wind and twenty-four hours of sun, we both wore goggles or glacier glasses at all times when outside the tent. Liv wore a contraption consisting of goggles and a plastic face guard attached underneath, which I referred to as her "Darth Vader" mask. I felt closed in by that style of mask, so I protected my face with a wrap I had made out of fleece with a wind-stop nylon layer, which I called "The Beak" because it did look ridiculously like a bird's beak. Each of us had a down sleeping bag and foam pad to sleep on.

Our first-aid kit was pretty standard for this kind of trek—an assortment of prescription painkillers, bandages for injuries ranging from blisters to gashes, and a suturing kit. I took a refresher session with EMTs before the trip to learn again how to suture large wounds. I didn't practice on real patients, but I had stitched up so many dead pigs' feet that I felt I could manage if either of us should be torn up. We also carried a repair kit for the inevitable problems we would encounter with equipment. The kit held a Leatherman multitool, safety pins, glue, screws, and tent and sail repair items, including extra sail fabric, parachute cord, duct tape, needles and thread, and buckles.

Liv and I each brought along a small bag for personal items. The bag carried the requisite things: toothbrush and paste, dental floss, wipes, sunscreen, heavy face moisturizer, toilet paper, and vitamins. (Liv brought her disgusting cod liver oil pills, which she swears are the cure for all ailments.) We also packed a few items of emotional significance. Liv carried a book of Norwegian poems, her journal, her envelope of notes from Einar, and her good-luck charm—a thumb-sized polar bear head carved out of bone). Over my years of polar expeditions and training trips, Pam and I have developed several traditions that allow me to take her with me on the ice. Pam is a woman of many talents; a graphic designer by trade, she is also a seamstress, writer, and artist. For every trip I make, she sews me a silk scarf that I wear as a base layer next to my skin. This expedition scarf was a kaleidoscope of colors, rich reds and purples, to remind me of the colorful world of home while I traveled amid the whiteness of Antarctica. I always use the same type of journal on these trips—a simple, hard-backed book with blank pages. After I had bought the books (one for the first leg to the South Pole, another for the last part of the journey), I turned them over to Pam for embellishments. She added endpapers and photos and pasted drawings inside the covers to remind me of her. For me, deciding what reading material to bring is always a tough call. Should I go with something I know and love, something I'll be happy to re-read, or take a risk on something new? This time around, my mom came up with an ingenious solution. She told Pam to ask each of a group of my close friends and family to choose a poem and send it to her. Pam printed those on thin, translucent vellum paper and bound them into a book with a hand-stitched binding. So I had a collection of poems, most of which I'd never read, that my friends and family had picked especially for me. Some included explanations of why they had chosen a particular poem, which were as much fun to read as the poems themselves. It wound up being a brilliant (and lightweight) way to carry my circle of loved ones with me.

I also carried a tiny beaded leather pouch on a string, a gift from one of my mentors, a former teacher of mine named Pat McCart. I first met Pat when I was in seventh grade at Summit School for girls. That was the year my dyslexia was diagnosed. The way the school decided to handle my learning difference was to pull me out of all my regular classes, along with one other girl. So I was tutored by an outside educator who was a specialist in learning differences. Then other teachers from the school volunteered to tutor us in subjects such as math and science. Pat was the one who volunteered to teach us science. When I look back on that intensive teaching, I realize that it made all the difference in the world. Of course, I hated it at the time—being separated from my peers, feeling different and less smart than the rest of the kids. I think Pat saw some of that. She could tell that some of the problems my learning difference was creating had more to do with self-esteem than with academics. I didn't feel I excelled in anything. So one day, Pat came in for one of our sessions and mentioned to me that she had heard I was a pretty good skier. It turned out that the teacher who was giving me math lessons, a roly-poly gal who was not exactly athletic, wanted to learn how to ski. So Pat asked me whether I would be willing to give her lessons. I was floored. A *teacher* wanted to learn something from *me*? During a school day the following week, the three of us met, and I spent the afternoon showing my math teacher the basics of downhill skiing. It was the first time in my life I had felt I had something to offer, the first time I realized that I possessed a skill or talent that someone else didn't. That day changed everything. Something clicked inside me and I finally understood that there was an entirely different world outside of school in which I could feel comfortable, a place where I could be a leader.

I transferred to public school for high school and lost touch with Pat. Then she contacted me in the 1980s, after I had gone to the North Pole. Shortly after that trip, I came out publicly as a lesbian, and Pat had read a story about that in the papers. She sent me a letter telling me that she was inspired by my courage in doing that. And she decided to come out publicly as well, which was a brave and pretty controversial step, especially for a principal at a private college preparatory school. The two of us became good friends and corresponded for a while.

In 1991 when I started to put the American Women's Expedition (AWE) together, I needed someone who would find a way to develop a curriculum for kids. I looked her up again. She wound up taking a year-long sabbatical from her administrative position to work with the expedition. She helped us find grant money to distribute to teachers around the country so that they could develop their own curriculum based on the trip. Then we took the curricula and gave them away to other teachers. We wound up with a pretty robust set of lessons for grades K–12. In an unpaid way, Pat was really our senior executive. We had bummed a model office from some office furniture company, so we had the use of a "showroom" they had set up in a big warehouse. We just had to leave whenever they wanted to bring by a prospective customer. The rest of the unheated warehouse was occupied by pigeons. I remember Pat sitting cross-legged on the desk, wearing her wool socks, just telling us that we could do this thing. Right before I left for Antarctica the first time, she gave me a small leather pouch, about the size of a fifty-cent piece, to take with me for good luck. I carried it across the continent with me. Shortly after I got back from AWE, just after my fortieth birthday, Pat died of cancer. I had her pouch with me on this trip, too, as a reminder of how much she had believed in me, as a way to tap into her strength and courage when I felt weak. It also reminded me, every time I fingered the worn leather in my palm, of what my life was about—making a difference in kids' lives the way that Pat had made a difference for me.

Even during the first few days of the trip, I could see how well Liv and I meshed as a team. It was wonderful to travel with someone who seemed to know what I was thinking without my having to say a word. We never discussed the need to make miles quickly; but during that first week, we both by silent agreement tacked a couple of extra hours onto each day in an effort to make up for the time we'd lost in Cape Town. The terrain for our first weeks included a gradual ascent along the Sigyn Glacier. The first day we were stuck using crampons because the ice was slick, blue, and hard. Blue ice is essentially ancient ice. It starts as snowfall that compacts over time so that the air between the flakes is squeezed out. Eventually—in five hundred years or so—it becomes so dense that it absorbs different light waves and appears blue. We couldn't sail safely on this terrain because it was too slippery, so we were forced to spend a fair amount of time towing our sleds. That first week, we were also treated to a couple of whiteouts, windstorms that kick up enough snow to block out the light and the horizon. I had forgotten how dizzying it can be to pull a sled in those conditions. I couldn't tell where the ground was, or which direction was straight ahead. It was bizarre to go from being able to see for miles into the distant horizon to being unable to see my own feet when I looked down. My compass became my eyes. I had to check its readings every few steps to make sure we didn't stray from our course. Peering into the pea-soup landscape, I would think I was following a perfectly straight line, but I would inevitably find that my disoriented senses were pulling me left or right. We made little progress on those days because one or both of us would get vertigo and we'd have to stop until the nausea and spinning sensation went away.

During the worst of these storms, when we couldn't see enough to take one step forward, we camped. We unrolled the tent from Liv's sled and popped it into its tunnel shape. We used tent stakes, ice axes, and ice screws to anchor the tent, and then shoveled snow and ice onto the tent flaps to weight it down. We drove our skis into the ice and then tied our sleds to them to prevent them from blowing away. If the wind was very fierce, we also tied the sleds to the tent as well. The whole process took from twenty to thirty minutes, and although it was done with mittens on, it was a race to make camp before our fingers lost all feeling. Once inside, Liv or I would light the MSR Stove™ to melt ice for water and to cook. It wouldn't take long before the tent was cozy with our body heat. The temperature inside the tent varied. If it were sunny, we might be able to sit in our sleeping bags wearing just our fleece jackets and fingerless gloves. But if it were blowing or particularly cold, we might be bundled up in our down pants and parkas. We used these cooped-up times to write in our journals or do our "homework." Years ago on my expedition to the North Pole, I had agreed to help a researcher from the University of Minnesota study the effects of isolation and stress on teams. Her research has been used by NASA to figure out how to prepare astronauts for missions. (The poles are strangely similar environments to outer space in terms of sensory deprivation and stress.) I had talked Liv into participating in additional research on this trip, so every Sunday night we had plenty of charts to fill out about our state of mind.

We had a range of equipment for different snow and ice conditions. On slippery blue ice we used the spiked crampons. We also had two sets of skis. One pair was skinny and lined on the underside with moleskin; we used those for pulling. Without the gripping of the moleskin, we would not have been able to tow sledges that were about twice our own body weight. We used wider "telemark" (downhill style) skis with steel edges for sailing.

With a few exceptions, sailing was pretty much a bust in those first weeks. When we did have good enough conditions to sail—decent wind and a relatively flat surface—the process proved to be much harder than it had been during our training trips. The wind could be incredibly strong. Dodging the sastrugi, the knee-high "waves" the wind had carved into the ice floor, while clipping along at 25 miles per hour (40 kph) was sometimes impossible. There were many moments when I was being tugged so hard by my sail that I was nearly sitting on my skis to keep my balance. The wear and tear on my knees and hips caused excruciating pain after crouching like that for an hour at a time, all the while using my legs as shock absorbers as I went over the bumps. We each had four sails—larger ones for lighter winds, smaller ones for strong, stormy winds. Dozens of lines of nylon cord ran from the sails to the steering bar attached to our waist harnesses. Often we would try one sail, only to have the lines tangle into a matted ball within minutes. Then we would either have to switch sails—if we had another that would work in the wind conditions—or spend an hour or more de-tangling the lines. It was tedious work that required exposing our bare fingers to the brutal cold.

Liv took the lead on the first sailing days, and watching her sled fly across the ice from behind was frightening. The winds here were gusty and inconsistent, pulling firmly but gently one moment, and then tugging violently the next. I am not as strong a skier as Liv, so I was working hard to get comfortable. This ski-sailing was unlike any of the practice trips we'd done. On our second day out on the ice, as we were still getting the feel of the sails, a huge gust caught Liv's 32-square-meter sail and pulled her off her feet into the air! She came down a half-second later, but the sail continued to drag her, her boots barely scraping the surface of the deep snow, for another 30 feet or so until she was able to pull her knife out of her jacket pocket and slash the lines. The knife was a type of switchblade, a present I'd given her in Cape Town because I think she would find it handy to have a knife she could open with one hand. It was a testament to Liv's quick-thinking and athleticism that she was able to fish the knife out of her pocket while managing the sail lines and keeping upright. As it turned out, that early incident proved an omen for our turbulent relationship with the wind: Throughout the expedition, it would alternately carry us, attack us, or desert us. But it left no doubt that we were completely subject to its whim. The fate of our trip would rest with the wind.

November 28, day 15, stands out in my mind as a particularly grueling one. The temperature was −30°F (−34°C), but the visibility was good and the wind light—excellent sailing conditions. We went up with the 15-square-meter sails at first and went about two minutes before a gust twirled Liv's sail into a matted mess of lines. We stopped, untangled that, and then three minutes later, my sail was tangled. We switched to the smallest storm sails and were off again. Everything was great, and then the line that tethered the sail to me snapped! The sail jerked forward, ripping the steering bar out of my hands and taking my mittens with it. My sail took off, swiftly tumbling off into the white. I quickly unhooked from my sled and skied after the billowing sail. I was panicked. I couldn't afford to lose that sail! I snapped off my skis and ran in my boots, gulping searing cold mouthfuls of air. The sail got hung up on a sastrugi; and then, as I was about to reach it, it flew off again. I glanced behind me, trying to keep my sled in sight. Finally, the sail had collected enough snow while sweeping along the ground that it collapsed on itself. I dove to my knees and came up hugging the sail to my chest. Liv, who was in the lead about 30 yards (27 m) ahead, turned around and saw me walking toward my sled with the sail in my arms. She had no idea what had happened. I had to walk backwards to my sled, the wind was so strong.

After regrouping and changing sails, we were up for fifteen glorious minutes—and then Liv's titanium tow bar broke. She killed the sail and looked at the damage. The two titanium bars that attached to each side of the sled, orienting it straight behind Liv, were twisted and bent. They were irreparable. For the remainder of the trip, she would have to go without a tow bar. So instead of pulling with a sled that was anchored on either side, forced to follow her at a set distance in a straight line, her sled was free to wiggle on a rope behind her, shimmying sideways or swinging out to the side when she hit sastrugi. We decided to camp for a while and rest; we had spent several hours on the ice, but only fifteen minutes of it sailing full speed. In that time, we had traveled almost 5 miles (8 km). That was great speed, but not much progress for the day.

Both of us had envisioned being able to sail like that for hours on end. We'd thought that by now, more than two weeks into the journey, we would be well on our way to the South Pole. Instead, we were just 88 miles (142 km) inland, with more than 1,100 (1,770 km) to go just to the Pole. Some of the miles we'd logged were also slightly off course, due to the wind direction. We could harness a crosswind and compensate to stay on course to some degree, but we still managed to put in a few miles that took us sideways. That night in the tent, I felt deflated. After dinner and writing in my journal, I lay on my back and peered out of my sleeping bag at the tent above. We'd started a record of each day's progress with a permanent marker on the ceiling fabric overhead. As I added up the scrawls of mileage to our paltry total, my first doubts began. Without voicing my fears, I knew that Liv could see our potential to fail written in the figures overhead as well. Doubt was to become our new companion, the unwelcome third guest on this expedition. It was a presence pointless to acknowledge, but a greater enemy than the cold or the ice. Those elements could eat away at us physically; but doubt would sap our mental and emotional strength. I sighed, thinking that we had a long way still to go. There was nothing to do but go to sleep now and try again the next day.

A few days after the accident with the emergency beacon, Ann and Liv reached the Polar Plateau. They had traveled 104 miles (167 km) into the continent in sixteen days, an average of 6.5 miles (11 km) a day—far fewer miles than they would have to travel each day to complete the journey in time. The temperature hovered around −30° F (−34°C). Already, the skin on Ann and Liv's faces had started to swell and burn from the wind and constant sun. Despite liberal applications of sunscreen and moisturizer, their skin still browned and peeled, leaving raw pink skin exposed to the elements. Their faces were swollen and wrinkled. Both looked like the grandmothers of the two women who had started the expedition. Once on the plateau, the wind picked up and the terrain flattened, so they were able to ski-sail for longer periods. By keeping their sails hoisted between three and five hours in a day, they started to gain 17 miles (27 km), and even as many as 35 miles (56 km) daily. Their after-dinner routine began to include several hours of sewing up tears in the sails or untangling "spaghetti" lines. Both of them were still getting used to the feel of the Antarctic wind and the various sails. But Ann, the slightly weaker skier, was feeling less confident than Liv. Ski-sailing in Antarctica was simply much more difficult than it had been in Norway and Canada where they had practiced. They had never traveled at the speeds they were attaining on the ice here, and the terrain was much rougher. Worse, the winds were rarely steady. Fierce, violent bursts of wind would interrupt a gentle breeze. They were forced to pick a sail that worked with dominant wind conditions, and then adapt to the variances with their bodies. They were also still experimenting with the rigging of the sail lines, trying to find the most efficient, comfortable, and safe way to tie the "kill" lines, which forced the sails to drop quickly if the women fell or wanted to stop.

On the afternoon of November 30, Ann and Liv were enjoying a strong, gusty wind. They had stopped sailing briefly to untangle their lines. Ann knew the line controlling the extra flap on her sail wasn't rigged properly, but she figured she would fix it during the next break. The line was supposed to feed into a pulley so that she could easily adjust her speed. Pulling the line in tightly drew the sail taut against the wind, increasing her speed. Letting the line out deflated the flap, allowing her to slow or stop. But Ann's flap line was looped around her tow bar twice before feeding into the pulley; essentially, her sail was stuck in full throttle. As she fiddled with her tangled lines, a gust of wind lifted her sail and began to pull her forward. She grabbed the flap line to let it out but had to first get enough slack in the line to un-loop it from her tow bar. She jerked hard on the line, just as another gust rushed into the sail. The force of the wind tore her arm outward, ripping a muscle in her right shoulder. Ann crumpled to the ground, her whole body convulsed in agony. Liv, who was several meters ahead, didn't see the reason for the fall, so she turned around and waited patiently, wondering why Ann was taking so long to get to her feet.

ANN

I lay on the ground for a good thirty seconds without moving. The pain in the front of my right shoulder was excruciating and felt as if someone had jabbed a hot poker into my body. Gritting my teeth, I gingerly rolled toward my right side and tried to push myself up by using my left hand only. It took me several minutes of struggling before I could maneuver myself off the ground. Once I was standing, I immediately went into denial about the pulsing pain in my shoulder. "It's just a strain," I said to myself. I waved to Liv, who was waiting up ahead. Then I hooked the steering bar around my left elbow and raised the sail. We were off again.

After that accident, every bump and sastrugi jolted pain through me. It felt as if the sail had partially ripped my arm out of its socket. I fought for an hour, crouched so low on my skis that I was practically eating the steering bar. We stopped for a break, some hot sports drink, and chocolate. I mentioned to Liv that I thought I had pulled something, but I gave no indication of how much pain I was in. I was still trying to figure out how bad the injury was, not wanting to scare myself or jump to conclusions. After our break, we doubled up because I was shaken by the fall: I sat on her sled as if straddling a horse, tied to my own. We went for thirty-five more minutes, and then stopped. The wind had shifted and was blowing us off course to the west. We briefly debated the merits of pulling for another hour, and then decided to camp. Taking a half-day rest would allow us to push harder the next day, when, we thought hopefully, better sailing conditions would return.

Liv and I rarely spoke while we made camp, but that afternoon my silence was steeped in disappointment. I felt I had let Liv down. I knew it wasn't fair for her to have to tow both of us. In fact, it wasn't going to be an option. She had strained her knee while towing me, an injury that led to a dull, aching pain which was to be with her for the remainder of the trip. I still had no idea how severely my arm was injured. I was in pain, but maybe after a good night's sleep, it would be reduced to stiffness. Never before had I been hurt badly on an expedition. For me, that had always been a point of pride. Years ago when I had trekked to the North Pole with Will Steger, I was secretly pleased by the media's shock when they learned that it was a male member of our crew who had fallen, damaged his ribs, and had to be evacuated, not me, the only woman, the one they had assumed would be the weakest.

I thought back to my trip to the South Pole in 1993. One of the women on my crew, Sunniva, had injured her ankle quite badly early into the trek. As we neared the Pole, she was in desperate shape. She'd been fighting bronchitis and a high fever for a few days. I remembered how frustrated I'd been. There was only so much I could do to help her without compromising my own physical health. And I saw her struggle emotionally to manage the pain: pushing as hard as she could to keep moving, and yet trying to pace herself so she that didn't have to quit completely. I'd known that was a fine line to walk, but I had not fully appreciated at the time the guilt she must have felt, the pressure she was under to come through for the rest of us, to succeed for our sakes. As I massaged my shoulder and downed two painkillers with a mouthful of water, I felt those emotions strongly for the first time myself. For the rest of the trek, I would have two jobs: one, to navigate the journey itself; the other, to manage my injury. It was a huge additional burden, one that took tremendous energy. And we were so early into the trip!

That night, the thought that I could fail was difficult, but the idea of bringing Liv down along with me was heartbreaking. I started to read from the book of poems that Pam had made for me. I got no further than the opening line of her note to me before the tears came hot and fast. My windwhipped nose stung when I wiped it. I rolled over so Liv wouldn't see me cry.

LIV

I knew Ann was badly hurt. I didn't see her fall, but her body language was unmistakable. She was in desperate pain. It is the nature of these trips that you are always aching in one way or another, always managing the toll the kilometers are taking on your body. But this was far beyond the level of typical discomfort that we take for granted on an expedition. Ann was an expedition veteran. I had to trust her to tell me if she needed to stop and rest. And yet, I thought she was in denial about how badly she was hurt. We made some more progress that day, logging about 16 miles (26 km) in all. I was worried about Ann, but I didn't know how to talk to her about it.

The next two days, we traveled swiftly and far, covering more than 66 miles (106 km). But we were stopping every half an hour or so to rest Ann's shoulder. I was challenged to stay warm during those breaks. I thought that it might be better for me to tow both of us when the wind was strong, so that we did not lose as much time. I was still in good condition, and though we could not travel quite as fast when I sailed for both of us, I was happy to do it rather than take frequent breaks or stop altogether. Though I knew I had to talk to her about the injury, I wasn't sure how. So my way of trying to show her that I knew she was hurt was to offer help. During our afternoon break, I walked over to Ann with a thermos and saw she was fumbling with getting unclipped from the sled. Without asking, I helped her release her harness. She blew up at me. "Listen!" she said. "I'm not one of the helpless tourists on your trips to Svalbard! I'm perfectly capable of managing on my own!" Ann had never spoken to me that way before, nor had I seen her explode like that at *anyone*. I was angry and hurt, but I also knew that she must be in awful pain to react that way. I set down the thermos and returned to my sled, counting my steps as I went to keep my temper in check.

I know how hard it is to admit to yourself that you are injured. Once, on a grueling expedition on Mt. Everest in 1996 with an international team of climbers, I nearly paid for my stubbornness with my life. Our team of ten was doing well. We were only two more camps away from the summit. I was terribly sick. I had a bronchial infection and had started coughing up blood. The only reasonable action was to descend as quickly as possible. I refused. I didn't want to let my team down. I didn't want to have worked that hard and still not reach the summit. As I sat down to rest, I was still in denial about how badly I was hurting. I thought I had sat down for only a few minutes, but it was actually closer to twenty. I remember being jolted to consciousness by a shocking sight: high above the place where I was resting, vultures were circling in the sky. These scavenger birds prey on the dead. I knew that for them to be looking at me as a prospective meal, I had to be close to death myself. That fear overcame my stubbornness. I got to my feet and descended to the next station, where I rested for a day or two. I made one more attempt to summit, but within 6,200 ft (1,900 m) of the summit, I was suffering so much from the altitude that I had double vision. At that point, I developed cerebral edema, a life-threatening illness caused by high altitude. The effects include swelling of the brain and hallucination. I wound up descending to base camp. My team summited days later, and I was not with them. Defeat is not easy to accept, but there are many things in life more important than winning. I knew that Ann had been hoping and trying to cross Antarctica for years. It would be hard for her to accept if her injury, or some other circumstance, forced us to give up. It would be hard for me as well. But I hoped that Ann would make good decisions, and that I would be able to help her keep perspective.

We sailed for another hour, making it four hours total, but we had to quit at 2:30 P.M. Ann was in too much pain to continue. We both set up camp in silence. It was my turn to cook, so Ann sat with the laptop and GPS, warming them up so we could check our position. I knew that Ann was ashamed of her outburst, but I was still frustrated about her words. I didn't want to talk about it, but I knew that I couldn't let the tension keep building. I finally just said to her, "Ann, I *know* you are capable, and I didn't mean to imply that you weren't. I'm just trying to be helpful because I know you are hurting."

She immediately apologized. I'm sure she noticed I was on the verge of tears. She said we had to find a way to talk about her injury and manage it. She said she had felt patronized when I tried to help her with the sail—she actually hadn't been having trouble with the harness at all. I let that sink in and then thought about how I would have felt if someone had tried to force unwanted help on me. We were quiet and serious for a moment. Then she said, totally deadpan: "Actually, I'm just trying to slow us down enough for Stannie to catch up so I can steal his seat." We both laughed, cracking the skin on our swollen, puffy faces.

That was the first time, but not the last, that we talked about Ann's injury. Still, it remained a difficult topic to navigate. As our trip progressed, I worried that Ann's fear of being the weaker one would drive us both to work harder than was prudent; she did not want to be the first one to give up in a day full of long hours of pulling. I found myself feigning tiredness sometimes to cut the pulling days short; I was concerned that we both remain fresh so that we could really push ourselves when the wind returned. But then I felt resentful that *I* looked like the weaker one. And, ironically, my attempt to be patient with Ann's fears around her injury was interpreted by her as a *lack* of patience on my part for the pulling. I think we misunderstood each other sometimes so thoroughly that we were almost on two different expeditions! Yet, I feel that we managed her injury better together after that first conversation. I guess even soul sisters can have their differences.

ANN

That night, I called Carolee Lindsey at *yourexpedition* and asked her to call my doctor to get his advice on how I should medicate myself from the first-aid kit to control the pain, yet not become too sleepy from the pain pills. I swore her to secrecy so that she wouldn't tell Charlie and the others. I didn't want them to worry about it because there was nothing they could do. But I finally admitted to myself the degree of the injury: It was a muscle tear, not a strain, and I wouldn't be able to stop using my shoulder long enough for it to heal. The best I could hope for was a few days of pulling to spell me from the ski-sailing. Otherwise, my only option was to pace myself, take pain pills, and hope it didn't get any worse. I felt awful for yelling at Liv. But I didn't want her pity. I knew that if we were going to make it, I had to let the injury be her problem and responsibility as well as mine—the same as I had done for Sunniva. But at the same time, it made no sense to me to risk injuring her knee further by letting her tow both of us. I could keep up. I *would* keep up. My greatest fear was letting Liv down. That night I wrote in my journal that I feared the possibility of failing her would haunt me for the rest of the trek.

In retrospect, my injury was a turning point in the journey in many ways. From that day forward, there was tension between myself and Liv that hadn't existed before. I was working hard to cope with the pain of the injury and not let it prevent us from moving forward. For her part, Liv was incredibly patient with me. And yet, we had frustrated conversations a few times: She wanted to help me in ways that made sense to her, like taking over my cooking duties or assisting me with sail lines. I kept trying to explain to her that those weren't the ways I needed help. While it didn't cause a rift between us, the injury became a source of low-level frustration. We are both stubborn women, so as much as she pushed help on me that I felt I didn't need, I pushed back to not accept it. Looking back, I think it is a testament to our friendship and our determination that we didn't allow that frustration to reduce us to arguing, or derail the journey. We both problem-solved—in ways that made sense to us at the time—around how to move forward and not drive each other crazy. But looking back, I am still stunned at the degree to which our experiences of the trip diverged at this point. I wish we had had the presence of mind to be more honest in the moment.

chapter seven

PUSH TO THE POLE

LIV

After Ann and I talked about her injury, we had good wind for three days. We covered more than 117 miles (188 km), sometimes sailing for six hours. We were both relieved to make some real progress, thrilled to see when we marked our position on the tent ceiling each night that we were making up for lost time. But the wear and tear of the sailing, especially for Ann with her injured shoulder, was terrible. Sailing at slower speeds was hard on the arms; but going faster was hard on the knees. We took five-minute breaks every thirty minutes so that she could walk around and rest her shoulder and stretch her knees. At night, it was hard for her to move her arm at all, and getting up when she caught a ski tip and fell was very difficult. She joked that she looked like a fish wiggling on the ice trying to flip herself so she could push up with her good arm.

The view in this region was mesmerizing. One day the color near the horizon was a dusky light blue that gradually deepened into a brilliant turquoise. Overhead, the sky matched the royal blue of our sails. The ice was flat on that day, so I was able to spend much of it gazing up in wonder without worrying about falling over a sastrugi.

I was in pretty good shape still. Though my knee was still bothering me, the elastic knee supporter I had brought was helping quite a bit. In the afternoons, the wind died down to the point where it was not worth sailing. We needed wind speeds of at least 5 meters per second (16 feet per second) for the wind to really pull us. We could still use wind a little slower than that to walk-sail without our skis on. That meant the sail was pulling hard enough to take some of the weight of the sled, which was still easier than towing.

One of my favorite things about sailing days was that I could sing as loud as I wanted and not even Ann could hear me. It was like having a private shower the size of an entire continent! During this time, I remember getting stuck on a song that was a celebration of our good fortune in the wind: *Vem kan segla forutan vind,* which means, "Who can sail without the wind?" in Swedish. As I am shy about my singing, most of my friends and family know me for my whistling instead. I am an incurable whistler. I do it all the time, to the point where I whistle unconsciously in some situations. One morning when it was my turn to make breakfast, I got up and went out to my sled to fetch something. As I dug through the sled's contents, I started whistling away without thinking. When I crawled back inside the tent, I heard Ann's muffled voice from inside her sleeping bag, "Liv, you know the tent fabric *is* pretty thin." So I guess we each had our ways of getting on the other one's nerves. My obsession with whistling started when I was young. I remember my grandmother catching me at it as a girl and reprimanding me because it was not a "ladylike" thing to do—and that I would never get married if I continued to whistle. So of course, after that, I whistled everywhere I went out of pure rebellion.

Those good sailing days were followed by a long and frustrating stretch of calm. We took advantage of the first day to repair our sleds and equipment. We had underestimated the damage the sailing would do to our gear. One of the thermoses—made of stainless steel—cracked open inside the bottom of my sled, spilling sports drink that immediately froze. We also spent hours sewing up tears in the sails. We wound up using up all our thread that week and had to start sewing with dental floss instead.

While the sailing was hard physically on Ann, the pulling was difficult for me mentally. I couldn't see the point of putting in the long days pulling, even though Ann seemed determined to pull every day until she dropped. For me, it made as little sense as a crew aboard a ship aiming to circumnavigate the world by getting out the oars when the wind died: Ultimately, those efforts wouldn't make enough of a difference to justify the expense of energy. I thought we should pace ourselves and rest when we lost the wind, so that we were fit and fresh to sail when it returned.

I had a very bad day on December 8. We woke to bitter cold, $-32°F/-35°C$, and we were reaching an area of high altitude as well. I began the day by walking too fast. My chest hurt, and I got a terrible headache. It felt as if my sled was filled with lead. That morning, my note from Einar had read, "Be careful. I love you!" It helped to have his words in my head as I trudged through the day.

The calm was bad for both of us emotionally. We were both starting to do the math: We needed to reach the South Pole in a little over a month if we were to have enough time left in the summer season to cover the second leg of the trip. We had been on the ice for twenty-nine days at this point, and we had covered 919 miles (1,479 km), averaging 32 miles (52 km) a day. The frustrating thing was that on good sailing days we had logged almost twice that. We just could not seem to get many days of wind in a row. The inconsistency of the wind made us nervous on the days when we were pulling, traveling as little as a few kilometers a day! On days like that, it was hard to stay focused on the ice underneath me and not think about when the wind would come. By luck, the note I pulled from Einar's envelope of messages on one of those long, pulling days was one that read, "Are you missing your tires?" He had drawn a funny stick-figure picture of me with three big tires tied behind me, a reminder of how boring I had found that part of the training. All that day, I thought about how much easier the pulling was because of that training.

Having had that experience made me more patient with the slowness of the movement and the weight. I started to think about how the ice around me was patient. It had been here for thousands of years, showing its age with brilliant shades of blue. I began to think of the patience of the cold air around me. How many centuries had this air swept along the ice, shaping the continent floor into gorgeous sculptures? With every step, I inhaled the cold air, taking it deep into my lungs, imagining my body absorbing its strong patience and then exhaling my anxious heat. My mind grew quiet and the kilometers slipped by. I slept well that night, untroubled by dreams of time passing quickly.

The next morning, December 9, while I was making breakfast, Ann told me she had decided we needed to "pull out all the stops" to rouse the wind. She had taken her pouch of lucky items from her teacher, Pat McCart, and hung it around her neck. She showed me some of what was inside: a rock from the railroad tracks near her house in Scandia (her little piece of home); a coin bearing the image of Sacagawea, the Native American woman who had guided explorers Lewis and Clark, two medallions from Liz Barrett, the teacher we met in Cape Town; some grains of rice that had been blessed by the Dalai Lama and taken by her friend Sue Giller up Mt. Everest; and a pebble from Robben Island, a piece of Nelson Mandela's strength, which she had collected at the beginning of our trip. Ann said we needed the magic of these items to bring wind. We are both superstitious in a half-serious way about these things. Ann's made-up term for that kind of magic or luck is "hoogity-boogity." "We need some hoogity-boogity today," she told me over oatmeal, raising her eyebrows imp-ishly and wiggling her fingers as if she were casting a spell.

That day, Einar's words to me were: "Family=Liv & Einar, Jannicke, Linn Christine, and Birgitte." I spent the day thinking about how Einar and his three daughters became my family. I first met Einar and his first wife in the early 1980s. They were part of the local ski club in Oslo where my boyfriend of the time and I trained. Einar's wife died sud-denly from heart failure related to asthma in 1985, leaving him with three girls, Jannicke (fourteen), Linn Christine (eleven), and Birgitte (six), to raise on his own. Later the same year, I split up from my boyfriend over many issues—among them my dreams of skiing across Greenland. I remember the morning when I knew that things between us would eventu-ally have to end. I had read in the morning paper that a fifty-eight-year-old man from Norway had skied across Green-land. I knew that if he could do it, then so could I. And I said so, out loud. My partner rolled his eyes and kept reading the paper. I felt my resolve harden and I remember thinking to myself that if this goal meant enough to me, the loss of a part-ner was not the worst thing that could happen. After the breakup, I spent three months trekking along the Himalayas in Tibet and Nepal.

At that point in my life, all my friends were married. My relationships would last for a year, or three years. And I was starting to wonder a little bit whether there was something wrong with me. My mother was worried. She thought that if I had a husband and a family, I would be happy. I just kept telling her, "That's not my life. I *am* happy." When I returned from traveling, Einar came courting. I moved in with him and the girls after three months, and we were married a few years later, when I was thirty-seven.

In the end I feel that it was good to wait and follow my heart. People say that I'm lucky to have Einar, and I am. But I made some very difficult choices early in my life when I was young and less confident, less sure of myself. I walked away from relationships that I really cared about but that would not let me be who I needed to be. I just couldn't seem to find a man who, instead of expecting me to be a home-maker, would be willing to let me be what I needed to become. I really wanted children at one point, but I was afraid of what would happen because I was so restless. I needed a partner who would be willing to share the domestic side of life, because I couldn't see myself giving up my career and sport. I had pretty much resigned myself to remaining single when I met Einar. He turned out to be that partner who would share, and he came with three great girls as part of the bargain as well.

I remember when I first moved in with Einar and his girls how shocked they were when I told them I couldn't cook. Of course, I knew how to cook, but I didn't enjoy it, and my idea was that they should be responsible for them-selves. It was, I think, a full year into living together before I cooked a meal for the family, and then they all made such a fuss. You would have thought it was Christmas, New Year's, and every special occasion wrapped into one. Thinking about that first meal I cooked for them made me smile as I trudged over the ice of Antarctica.

ANN

As much as I was frustrated when the wind disappeared in early December, I was also a little relieved. Pulling at least made completely *different* parts of my body hurt, so I could spell the shoulder. At the end of a day spent pulling for six or ten hours, my elbows ached from the repetitive motion of striking my ski poles into the ice—to test the ice for crevasses. My hips were sore from bearing the weight of the sled. But mercifully, my shoulder felt better. I had been able to manage it so far by taking frequent breaks when we were sailing, not letting it get stressed to the point where I couldn't move it anymore. I was pretty sure that I would be able to hold out long enough to finish the trek.

The good news was that I was becoming more adept with the sails. Both Liv and I were making changes to the way our lines were rigged and the way we handled the steering bars to make sailing easier. I had also named all my sails. By this time, each seemed to have its own unique personality. Learning how the sail responded to changes in wind speed and direction and the shifting of my weight or grip were just like getting to know a person. My storm sail, the smallest of the four, I named after Pam. It was tough and tiny, just like her. My 15-meter, I named after my cousin, Liz Field. Liz was diagnosed with breast cancer the month or so before I was to leave for Cape Town. I would think of her each day. In the early days of sailing, I struggled with this sail. It was so fierce and strong. I felt as if the sail and I were fighting these tough, tough winds. It reminded me each day of Liz and the battle she was fighting. I figured I could hang on a little longer because her "winds" didn't really ease up. I named the 15-meter with the flap sail "Puddin' Pie" after my nickname for Morgan, my very stubborn niece. At that time, she was two years old, and we were already best buddies. I marveled at how distinctly I could already see her personality emerging. There were so many times when she would completely wipe out, get the wind knocked out of her, or bump her head. But she would stand there biting her lower lip, absolutely refusing to cry. That 15-meter with the flap sail was the same way, doing whatever it wanted to do no matter how I coaxed and pulled it.

I named the triangular sail, called a NASA sail, for its resemblance to the wings of the U.S. space shuttle, after Dorothy MacIntyre, one of my staunchest supporters. I first met her after my American Women's Expedition (AWE). She was well-known in Minnesota for the big role she'd played in lobbying to get Title IX legislation passed. So I told her about my high school crusade and we had that battle in common. Over the years, she's taught me plenty about perseverance and grace. She looks like a teacher from the 1950s, very ladylike and polite. But she has this incredible quiet strength and a compelling way of enlisting others under her leadership— such as the way she persuaded a fleet of male college athletic directors to support Title IX. Her choice was either to alienate them or to bring them into the fold, and she did the latter. She never quit, but she never burned bridges, either. She had a quiet kind of power that was not flashy. She seemed deceptively unintimidating—you wouldn't look at her and think she was a dynamic, powerful woman who was making huge change. The same was true of my NASA sail. It could pull you along gently and seem perfectly benign. But it had this tremendous hidden power that could kick up in an instant.

The NASA was by far the hardest sail to handle, but was also the best to use in light winds. The tiniest breeze would catch this triangular 32-square-meter sail and pull us along. But unlike the rectangular sails, which would immediately "deflate" if Liv or I fell, it was difficult to get the NASA sail down. When it was in the air, one long edge faced forward; our lines were connected to the other two sides of the triangle, and then the point in between those two sides faced backward. We eventually attached an extra kill line to that tip, which we lashed to our steering bars. When you fell using the NASA, it would drag you—over sastrugi or whatever was in your path—until you managed to grab that line and reel it in.

December 16 kicked off a crazy, four-day run that I dubbed the "rodeo." We entered an area where the ice undulated into three-and four-foot high sastrugi for miles in every direction. The winds were strong, pulling us along at between 7 and 10 mph (11 and 16 kmph). It was like skiing very fast downhill over constant moguls. Both of us kept catching our ski tips and winding up sprawled on the ice, new bruises forming under our layers of down. Without a tow bar to stabilize it, Liv's sled regularly flipped over in the air while she was sailing and crashed down on its contents. Sometimes she could get it to flip back over on the next sastrugi. Sometimes she had to stop to right it and tighten the straps. I kept imagining that if we'd had a third person to shoot video of the two of us, the footage would be set to a twanging banjo-picking song, like something from the car chase scenes in the *Dukes of Hazzard* television show. Yee Haw! Look at 'em go! My knees took a beating, as did Liv's. But oh, the miles we made: 54, 65, 46, 64 (87, 105, 74, 103 km). Each day the totals on the tent ceiling made me smile big over my soup.

After the first day of rodeo, we called into base camp and talked with Zoë Alderfer Ryan, our education program director. She had news for us about the teachers and kids who were using our journey in their classrooms. A group of fifth-graders in Quito, Ecuador, had joined our mileage challenge and were trying to "beat" us across the continent! Some senior citizens in Palo Alto, California, had started meeting a couple of times a week at their local McDonald's to track our progress. These folks would then take updates about us into the local schools where they were volunteers. Students from John F. Kennedy High School, an inner city school in the Bronx, New York, were comparing the journal snippets Liv and I were sending to our Web site with the journals of historic figures, such as Leonardo da Vinci. They were using the journals, along with the "Dare to Dream" curriculum, as a model for setting and fulfilling goals, dreams, and objectives. Hearing about the international response was a tonic to my poor knees. Hell, I could hold out for months on the rodeo if these were the results we were getting!

We hit 80° south on December 18 and celebrated that night in the tent with shots of Aquavit. Our enthusiasm was slightly dampened by news from Einar that the Norwegian press was reacting pretty negatively to our slow progress.

They weren't even covering the angle of the education program there. Later Liv learned that the Norwegian department of education had not informed teachers there that the curriculum had been translated into Norwegian. It was finally released to teachers through a Web site during our last week on the ice. Liv was understandably indignant—especially as we'd gone to the extra trouble to run the curriculum past several consultants to make sure it wasn't too "American" for Norway.

We were cheered the next day by our first interview with CNN's Daryn Kagan, though. I'd met Daryn at one of my lectures before Liv and I started the trip. She was eager to stay in touch and see what we could put together from the ice. Again, we were indebted to John for getting hold of that phone. Although the viewership of CNN isn't huge, the key thing is that it's on in newsrooms all over the world; this meant that all the other major media outlets were aware of how we were progressing even if they weren't covering us—yet. Of course, I had no sense of that while I was on the ice.

We made the most of what was to be our last day of good wind by crunching our breaks down into the tiniest time slots possible. I started to refer to them as "pee, chew, and fly" breaks. We'd done the calculations on our food rations and it turned out that we were carrying more food than we needed. Both of us were going through about 4,000 calories a day, less than we had budgeted for the trip. So we decided to dump some of our food, just oatmeal and sports drink powder. (We didn't leave any of the packaging, just the food itself.) That night, Liv spoke on the satellite phone with a school in Norway that the two of us had visited when I was with her on a training trip in Mølladammen, Norway. I couldn't understand a word of the conversation, but I could hear the excited voices of the kids chirping through the satellite phone. Liv smiled and laughed as she chatted with them, promising (she later told me) to come visit them again after the trip was over. We both went to sleep that night with our spirits high, feeling that we were back on track. That feeling would not last long.

LIV

The wind died shortly before Christmas, leaving blustery whiteout in its wake and two very depressed women. Each morning, Ann and I would wake up and anxiously listen for the wind. Christmas Eve day, we walk-sailed for seven hours, gaining a little more than 16 miles (26 km). We decided to try to lift our spirits that night by celebrating the holiday. I was very excited about giving Ann the gift I had brought. While I was in Norway, I had a mouth harp made for her, with its own little wooden case. The harp looks like two metal question marks facing each other, with a reed in between. It uses the mouth as a sound chamber, and as you twang the reed, you can change the sound by changing the shape of your mouth. I also had one made for myself. Ann was delighted with the gift, and we stayed up late that night composing songs on our instruments, hoping to bring what both of us really wanted for Christmas—more wind.

ANN

I really blew it with my Christmas present for Liv. For my Christmas in Antarctica with the women from AWE, I got a kick out of trying to see what kind of ingenious small gift I could stash in my bags or make to cheer my teammates. I surprised the team by dressing up like Santa Claus and giving out gifts. I had red long johns, and then I took a bit of stuffing out of one of the sleeping bags for a beard. I had brought special foods for a Christmas meal: dried eggs with dried green and red peppers. I gave Sue Giller my extra pair of unworn socks. I had asked all the women's partners to write a letter, which I'd saved for the occasion. I made an Indian "dream catcher" out of Q-tips for a gift. The whole thing was silly, just a gag to boost everyone's spirits. But it was a hoot.

For some reason, with Liv's gift, my creativity utterly failed me. I had bought some beautiful handmade chocolates for her while we were in Cape Town, thinking they would be a great gift. For some reason, I completely failed to take into account that by the time Christmas arrived, the two of us would've been eating chocolate every day for weeks and weeks! She did like the gift and they were delicious—just not nearly as special as I'd intended them to be when I thought of the idea. Liv had me way outfoxed in the gift-giving department. The mouth harp was fantastic.

We each checked in with family and some of the crew the next day. Liv and I had arranged to give Norwegian wool sweaters to everyone on the team. Charlie was on the phone for a brief moment giving me grief about shooting more video footage. He wanted to make sure that we had some use-able shots to send back from the Pole once we got there. It was hard for Liv and me to take the breaks we needed to shoot footage. Shooting while sailing or pulling was pretty near impossible; you needed your hands for other things. And the time it took (not to mention the body heat you lost) to stop and shoot was tough to justify. Charlie also teased that I shouldn't let "One-Eyed Liv" near the camera, a joke from her solo trek to the Pole. One of her media sponsors had given her a digital camera to take with her, but it was hard to use, and there was obviously no one to take pictures of Liv, since she was alone. So she had held the camera pointed at herself and talked, giving updates on conditions and the trip. When she got back to Norway and turned over the tapes to her spon-sors, they came back to her in disbelief: There wasn't one usable shot taken inside the tent. In every tape, Liv had man-aged to frame the picture in such a way that it included just one of her eyes, and that was it. Once Charlie heard that story, he had coined the nickname "One-Eyed Liv," and hadn't let her live it down. But, not to be outdone in the teasing and practical jokes, Liv had *more* than gotten even with him (and snookered me as well) before we left for Cape Town.

While I was working with the team to secure stateside corporate sponsors, Liv was heading up the efforts to get our sails made. She began working with a sail maker in Norway named Eva Fischer—one of the few people in the world and the only woman who practices the craft for this purpose—to custom-design the sails. Eva would piece together different-sized and -shaped sails, and then Liv and I would test them at her cabin in the mountains in Hallingdal to see which construction handled better. Shortly before we left for Cape Town, Liv sent digital photos of the final versions of the sails to Charlie and me via e-mail. I remember opening the photo and gasping in disbelief. There on my computer screen was a photo of Liv, smiling and holding one of our royal blue NASA sails in her outstretched arms. But emblazoned across the sail—instead of Volvo's slogan, "Volvo for Life"—was the phrase "Volvo for *Liv.*" I knew Charlie would be freaked. The team had already packed for the trip to Cape Town and we didn't really have time to have the sail re-made. I walked over to Charlie's cube and asked whether he'd checked his e-mail. He simply moaned in reply, "What are we going to do?" The two of us really sweated about how we would handle it with Liv. We had a long conversation about whether a strategically placed patch with the word "Life" might throw off the balance of the sail, or make it less effective. We were stumped as to how to fix the problem. Finally, Charlie called Liv and explained her mistake. He put the phone on speaker so that I could help him figure out what to say. Liv picked up on the second ring.

"Hey, Liv. It's Charlie. How's it going?"

"Great, great. Did you get the photo I sent of the sail?"

"Yeah. . . . Um. . . . We did."

"Doesn't it look terrific?"

"Well. . . . See . . . here's the thing," Charlie stammered.

And at once, Liv was laughing uncontrollably on the other end of the line.

"Gotcha," she said.

The photo was a fake. The sail had had the right slogan all along. Charlie and I both had to laugh about being bested so thoroughly.

The pressure climbed for Liv and me as the days slipped into the new year. We had decided that we had to make the Pole by January 17 to have enough time left to finish our journey.

New Year's Day was a great sailing day, but again it was torture for me. We logged more than 40 miles (64 km) in nine and a half hours, most of it sailing in whiteout conditions. We could barely see a thing. During the last two hours, I was in so much pain that I thought I was going to throw up. I barked at Liv when she tried to help me unhitch from my sled during one of our breaks. But when we finished the break I pulled myself together enough to accept her offer to lead. That night in the tent, I thought about Charlie and the rest of the team. They had all invested so much time and energy and emotion in our trek. I felt lucky to have them all pulling for me back in Minneapolis. I felt lucky to have them all as friends.

The next day, we pulled during a whiteout. But Liv grew nauseous after four hours, so we decided to stop. Whiteout can be so confusing. It's as if you were a cartoon character dropped onto a white page. You have no sense of direction. You put a foot forward and you're not sure where the ground is. It's amazing to think how much one's movement is cued by sight. Without that information, the body doesn't know how to process the input. We made 10 miles (16 km) that day. It was my turn to cook, so I asked Liv to grab a bag of dinners out of her sled. She came back to the tent and said, "I don't have any left. They must be in your sled." That was strange. I went out to check my sled: no dinner bags. A quick survey of both sleds confirmed that we were one bag short. We had left it back in Cape Town during all the confusion of moving locations. I went through the remaining food bags and reassessed, counting portions. It turned out we had more than enough *calories* to get us through to the Pole—but it would be mostly in oatmeal and chocolate. We split one of our two remaining dinners that night. I thought of all the times that I had joked that I could live on chocolate. I was about to see if that were true.

To appease Charlie, Liv and I set up the camera on top of an overturned cooking pot inside the tent on January 3. We taped ourselves doing another interview with Daryn Kagan of CNN, but we didn't have much happy news to report. We were stuck in whiteout that day, cooling our heels in the tent until we could move safely. Poor Daryn had her work cut out for her to make the segment exciting, so apparently the producers decided to jazz it up by having a meteorologist comment on the weather in Antarctica. Liv and I stifled giggles while the meteorologist talked to us over the phone about the weather patterns that we were sitting in. After the interview, we decided to give a concert demonstrating our mouth-harp skills. Actually, Liv's mouth harp skills. I decided to spare the base camp crew my meager talents at that stage. So Liv started playing a "wind song," and I started waving my hands and head with the rhythm, sort of "dancing" while sitting in my sleeping bag. We were both punchy and tired after days of waiting for wind, so it wasn't long before the two of us just lost it. Liv complained with mock outrage to the camera about my pathetic "dancing." "Look at this! I am trying to create fine art and she is making fun?!!" At some point, in between the laughter, I signed off, telling the crew that we missed them, but we were sure that after watching this video they wouldn't be missing us. John later told us that when the team saw that footage, they were sure we had been tipsy on Aquavit.

A few more days of low mileage and whiteout, and Liv and I were feeling pretty desperate. We couldn't ignore the growing possibility that we might not make the Pole in time. We set up a call with Charlie and John in Minneapolis to discuss the situation. By our calculations, Liv and I would run out of food if the journey stretched past the twentieth. A food-drop from a plane would be possible, but at that point, the drop would be more about survival than continuing the journey; we wouldn't have enough time left in the summer season for the second half of the trek if we didn't make the Pole by the seventeenth. Charlie and the rest of the team were more worried about the food situation than Liv and I were. We had plenty of fuel to melt ice, and we could go a long way on that alone. Besides, we had enough calories, just not many dinners. Having to eat chocolate and oatmeal for a couple of weeks was annoying, but no tragedy. What I really wanted was wind. But we did have to discuss different scenarios—what we would tell the press, how we would work logistics for getting off the Pole. Liv and I were both solemn as we listened to Charlie run through the possibilities. We both wanted so much for the expedition to be a success. And the weight of the hope and expectations of all the people we'd brought on our journey was far heavier than our sleds at this point. We were terrified that we might disappoint them.

That night, I wrote in my journal about Shackleton. Despite all of the acclaim he received after his miraculous survival in Antarctica, he never got what he wanted from that cold white continent. He died on a ship in 1921 during his fourth trip to the continent, an attempt on his part to circumnavigate the continent. Shackleton said, "We all have our own White South." He was saying we all have dreams that drive us, that lure us. For him, Antarctica was as much an inner, mental landscape as it was a real place. I wrote that I thought it was sad he hadn't been satisfied with the inner journey he'd taken with his men on the trip in 1914–1916, but instead had continued to pursue the physical goal until it consumed him.

I wondered how I would feel if I had to stop at the Pole. That would for me be two incomplete versions of my dream. There was much in those two journeys that I was proud of. Would I have the strength and integrity to be satisfied with what I *had* achieved? Or would the crossing become an elusive goal I chased beyond all reason, as Shackleton had done, even to the exclusion of getting on with the rest of my life?

Finally. Our "hoogity-boogity" kicked in on January 10. We awoke to gusty winds at 5:00 A.M. By 7:30 A.M., we had packed and were on our way. Had a few false starts; Liv got a tangle and I got dragged for a bit with the NASA. We changed to the 15-meter sails and flew: almost 70 miles (113 km) in ten hours, our biggest gain yet. We followed that up with a few good solid sailing days, a short break in the wind, and then an amazing marathon sail. During that time, I had my most dangerous encounter yet with sailing. I was tracking behind Liv on January 12. We were sailing at a good clip, probably close to 9 mph (16 kph), using the NASA sails. A huge gust of wind came up just as I was at the top of a ramp-like sastrugi. I launched into the air. I felt my harness jerk and lift me up, and suddenly I was looking down at the ground, more than 7 feet (2 m) below my skis. My sled dangled from my harness, the end barely touching the ground. I hung there for almost three seconds, and then crashed back to the ice in a heap and was dragged for several yards. I was incredibly lucky. No broken bones. But I was terribly shaken. Liv, who had missed the whole thing, eventually noticed that I had fallen and stopped to let me catch up. I wasn't going anywhere until I changed to a smaller sail, which I did, and then we were on our way again. Later, during one of our breaks, I told Liv about the incident, which we both referred to thereafter as my "Mary Poppins moment."

The next day, fueled by chocolate, desperation, and four hours of sleep, we sailed for more than fourteen hours, getting within a day's striking distance of the Pole—just 20-some miles (32 km). I could see the line of jet exhaust in the distance. Elated, I followed the Habermans' directions to call the *Today* show first for the exclusive. We were going to make it. The journey would continue! An intern answered the phone at NBC. I explained that I was calling from Antarctica and that we were almost at the Pole. She put me on hold for a few minutes and then returned to the line, sighed and said, "Well, could you us call back when you get there? And don't call anyone else!" Good grief. Once again, the clarity of the phone belied the distance of the call, as well as the effort it took to make it. Every time I made a media call, I had to ski or pull with the phone and its battery inside my coat to keep them warm. I also had to check the time constantly and then work our breaks and eating in around the call. I had to remember to carry the right numbers with me somewhere in my parka where I could get to them quickly. And all the preparation was topped off by having to stop and stand still in the cold and *take my mittens off to dial!* Basically, I was risking fingers to make the phone call, and this woman was brushing me off as if I were a telemarketer. Sheesh!

A few hours later, we sailed into the South Pole compound, where it was 4:00 A.M. on January 16. Pretty much everyone was asleep. As we struggled out of our harnesses, a researcher popped out from one of the buildings to take some weather readings. He started when he saw us, but had no doubt been anticipating our arrival. He looked at his watch and smiled, "Well, you two are here early, aren't you?" Liv and I exchanged glances. Early! We were barely in time.

⌒ ⌒ ⌒

As the South Pole station began to stir, Ann and Liv were greeted by Katy Jensen, a friend of John Tuttle's who worked at the Pole. She persuaded the cafeteria to open early, and the two adventurers savored their first hot breakfast of fresh food (and non-chocolate) for weeks. The crowd around the two explorers grew as other "Polees" joined the table to hear the stories about their trek. Exhausted, Ann and Liv gamely answered questions and gorged.

Back in Minneapolis, the team had been tracking Ann and Liv's GPS position for hours. In anticipation of the call from Ann and Liv at the Pole, Charlie had gathered a few journalists in the *yourexpedition* offices. The media crowd hovered around the conference room impatiently while a cameraman lined up a shot of the phone itself.

"Shouldn't they be there already?" Charlie asked John. John made a call to his friend Katy, and after spending a few minutes on hold, spoke with two very full, very sheepish explorers. Distracted by the excitement of reaching the Pole, and disoriented from their first encounter with "room temperature" and other humans in weeks, the two had completely forgotten that the team was waiting for them to call. They dutifully (if somewhat tardily) answered reporters' questions, and then made several phone calls to other media outlets around the world for prearranged interviews. After quick showers and more introductions, Ann and Liv rested. Over the next day, they would re-pack their sleds, give a lecture about their trip to the scientists and staff at the Pole, and prepare for the second half of the journey.

The Amundsen-Scott South Pole Station is home during the summer months to about 125 people, a mix of scientists and facilities staff. Run by the U.S. National Science Foundation (NSF), the station is home to scores of research projects exploring climatic change, atmospheric change, geology, and astrophysics. During the winter, when the average temperature drops to −58°F, the Polee population drops to about 30 people, a skeleton staff willing to tough out a winter of complete darkness.

The base was named after the two explorers who had raced each other to be the first to discover the South Pole in 1911: Roald Amundsen, a Norwegian, and Robert Falcon Scott, a Brit. Scott, who came across the Pole just a month after Amundsen had staked his claim, arrived to find Amundsen's tent, a letter inside addressed to the king of Norway, and a note asking Scott to please deliver it. Although Amundsen's crew made it safely back to their camp and then telegrammed the world to announce victory, Scott and his four men perished on their return trip out of the continent's interior. Scott continued to write in his journal to the bitter end, and wound up documenting what has become one of the most famous examples of gentlemanly heroism (and British understatement): One of Scott's men, Titus Oates, a British army officer who had suffered for weeks with frostbitten feet, decided to sacrifice himself for the good of the expedition. He woke up one morning and told Scott, "I am just going outside and may be some time." With that, Oates walked out of the tent into the blizzard and to his death. Scott wrote: "We knew it was the act of a brave man and an English gentleman. We all hope to meet the end with a similar spirit, and assuredly the end is not far."

The establishment of a base at the South Pole was somewhat of a race as well. The station was built by the Americans in 1956 during the cold war, mostly to prevent the Russians from building there first. The original 1956 building is now buried under 30 feet (9 m) of drift snow and ice and is slowly being crushed from all directions by enormous pressure from the Polar Plateau. In the same way that oceans have patterns of flow and current, so does the ice of Antarctica. The flow is just too slow to be visible. Because the South Pole is downs-lope from Titan Dome to the southeast, the ice at the Pole and everything on it—including buildings, vehicles, and people—is flowing 29 feet (9 m) a year, roughly northwest. Each year the marker for the South Pole must be moved to account for the shift in the ice.

Abandoned in 1976 for the new Amundsen-Scott station (built by the United States Navy), the Old South Pole was left nearly intact, even down to the mess hall tables still set for diners who would never arrive. When Liv visited the South Pole in 1994, the juice machine at the current mess hall broke; a team of Polees was dispatched to the Old South Pole station (still accessible through various tunnels) to scavenge the old, still perfectly good juice machine.

ANN

I think that visiting the South Pole would be a slightly sur-real experience under any circumstances. Having just spent two months isolated in the icy desert of the continent's inte-rior, for Liv and me, our time there bordered on bizarre. I thought that, because I'd been to the Pole before, the approach to it would seem familiar. But the ice is so vast that even a group of buildings as large as the station appeared tiny on the horizon. We saw it as a speck in the distance, and then it bobbed in and out of view as we dipped into slight valleys. The station was so tiny for so long that I kept thinking the speck couldn't possibly be it. But sure enough, as we drew closer, we saw big puffs of jet exhaust from the planes taking off of the runway.

We dropped our sails right in front of the ceremonial South Pole—the red- and white-striped pole surrounded by the flags of the nations that signed the Antarctic Treaty. Much had changed at the Pole campus since my last visit years ago. A giant construction project to upgrade the Pole facilities had begun in the meantime. Three new buildings on high stilts (to prevent them from being covered over by drifting snow) were nearing completion to provide a new generator system, new spaces for research labs, and additional living space for the community. The next day, the sound of forklifts backing up and the whir of power tools would replace the silence of the last sixty-four days.

Going from the almost complete sensory void of the inner continent to the bustling Pole was a jarring experience to say the least. We entered the Geodesic Dome, essentially a large unheated canopy that protects the buildings inside from being covered with snowdrift, by descending a wide ramp. Inside the dome were long rows of trailers, as well as several buildings. Katy took us to the mess hall, where, for Liv and me, the heat was oppressive. My eyes immediately began to water. I didn't get a good look at anything for a couple of hours while they adjusted to room temperature again. The smells were overwhelming—food, cleaning products, diesel fuel, and, as we began to warm up, our own bodies. And if the sensory overload was disorienting, the social overload was positively dizzying. It had been so long since I'd had a conversation that my brain seemed to be in slow motion. It was great the people there were so excited about talking to us and asking us questions. But I felt as if I'd been cornered by the paparazzi. To me, it was no wonder that the two of us lost track of time and our focus. When someone came to let Katy know she had a phone call, Liv and I were like, oh, yeah. Let's talk to the team. We were on such a different wavelength. And then, once we had talked to them, we realized—oh, *right*! This was a big milestone that the press was waiting to hear about. We should have called right away. I think that to some degree, for Liv and me, our arrival at the Pole was anticlimactic because we'd already been there. Crossing that threshold and beginning the second half of the trip would be our real milestone.

The South Pole is not in the business of providing accommodations to expedition teams, so we pitched our tent close to the ceremonial Pole. It felt as if we had picked Grand Central Station. Throughout the night (still bright as day), soon-to-depart South Pole staff came out near our tent to snap souvenir photos, waking the two of us up with their chatter and greetings.

We spent a fair amount of time socializing with various researchers and scientists who were curious about our trip. To some extent, the Pole is conducive to striking up deep friendships quickly. It is such a strange environment in which to meet people—isolated inside a freezer where there is constant daylight—that the camaraderie tends to be instantaneous. We enjoyed meeting everyone, but we were relieved to retreat to our tent to snap our own photos and write postcards to sponsors, friends, and loved ones back home.

In addition to all the requisite photos we took of ourselves by the ceremonial Pole and the flags, we also had a very important request to fulfill. Months before, when Liv and I were training in Norway just outside Oslo, we were privileged to have an audience with the Dalai Lama, the spiritual leader of the Tibetan people. Both Liv and I have deep respect for this man, and we were thrilled by the chance to meet him. He was in Oslo giving a speech at a hotel amphitheater. We had tickets to the speech, and as Liv had a friend who was the head of the Tibetan Society in Oslo, she asked if we might meet his holiness in person. Her friend pulled a few strings and was able to make arrangments for us join a group of Westerners for a question-and-answer session at the hotel. So we found ourselves in a little conference room listening to the Dalai Lama for about half an hour while he answered questions about the political situation in Tibet and China. Everyone in the room was just spellbound. Too soon, it was over and he had to meet with another group. He and his entourage of protectors and interpreters, all dressed in robes, filed out. We were able to shake his hand as he left, a completely exhilarating experience.

Liv and I hung around for a bit so that we could thank her friend. And then Liv got bold and asked whether it would be possible to have a photo taken with his holiness. She said that as we were headed to Antarctica and had organized an educational program for kids, it would be great to have his blessing. So Liv's friend went to talk to the guys in the robes and returned to tell us that he had no idea how long the next group would take, but that we should wait. Someone offered up a camera if we should actually get this chance for the photo. I was anxious, thinking we had already taken up too much of the Dalai Lama's time. But Liv is gutsier than I am, and she insisted that we stay. Next thing I knew, the Dalai Lama and his entourage were filing out of the conference room past us. He bowed, and we bowed, and then he headed for the door. Then, just before he exited, one of his aides grabbed his elbow and whispered something into his ear. Lo and behold, he turned around and made a beeline for us. In a second, he had grabbed our hands with both of his and embraced us. I was about falling over with the awe of being in the presence of such greatness. I could barely find my tongue when he asked us about the education program and the kids. He posed for a picture with us, drawing both of us in tight with a hug. He said goodbye and headed again for the door. Then he stopped, turned around and pulled a white prayer scarf out of his aide's bag. He held it to his forehead and blessed it, and then asked us whether we would take it with us and fly it at the South Pole. We agreed, and he explained how it should be flown correctly. Then he bowed, hugged us, and was gone.

We were on cloud nine, so incredibly honored to have had the chance to meet this great man and then to have the privilege of fulfilling his request! At one point on the ice, Liv and I had made some comment on the phone in one of our check-ins about the prayer scarf and the small Tibetan flag that Liv had brought with her for good luck. There wasn't any political commentary in it. But apparently, some muckety-muck at the South Pole got bent out of shape and worried that we intended to stage a protest for the Tibetan people at the Pole. They made a big hoopla, called our host Katie at the Pole, and instructed us NOT to fly that scarf or flag. They were concerned that somehow we were going to do something that made them look as if they were taking political sides. So Liv and I did just what we have both done all our lives when someone in authority tells us we can't do something: We ignored it.

While we camped next to the giant red-striped pole, we waited till the middle of the night when everyone on the station was sleeping. Then we crept out of our tent and kept our promise to the Dalai Lama, flying both the flag and the scarf, and capturing it in a photo to send back to him with our thanks and good wishes.

LIV

Being back at the Pole brought a rush of memories from my first visit. I remembered the warmth of the people here, their dedication to their work. I remembered that I felt I was floating on air, I was so happy to have achieved my goal. Six years seemed like so little time, and not much had changed. When I arrived at the Pole in 1994, one of the common questions I was asked was, "What does your husband think of this trip?" I noticed that nobody asked a male Japanese skier, who had made the same trek at nearly the same time as I did, what his wife thought of his journey. The reaction back home in Norway was sometimes more harsh. A couple of newspapers wrote the story as if I had abandoned my children for the trip: "Mother Leaves Children Behind in Trek to Pole" was one of the headlines. That was silly, of course, because even the youngest of the girls was well into school age before I made the trip. The oldest one was a teenager capable of caring for herself! And Einar, who had been taking care of them for years, was still with them. Still, people had funny ideas. I remember also that some people were surprised to meet Einar and see that he was an ambitious man with his own interests and goals. They had assumed that he must be a couch potato bum for his wife to be going off on all these trips. I made it a point after that trip to bring Einar up in my interviews, because I think that men need to know that partnering with a strong woman doesn't mean that they are weak, or that they will lose their own ambitions. I found that just as many people asked me this time around what my husband thought of my adventure. Even six years later, I was still a bit of an oddity.

Because it is a research station, everyone at the Pole is friendly, but they are not allowed to give you "official" help. Ann and I still slept in our tent there, and our use of the showers and cafeteria was as guests of individuals there, not as part of South Pole policy. These rules came about because the station did not wish to be accused of helping too much or unequally. And, mainly, it did not want to become a Motel 6 for explorers. But the people there were enthusiastic and curious. They wanted to hear all about how we sailed, how we pulled our sleds. They were especially grateful when we left several boxes of our extra chocolate behind, a treat they do not get often at the South Pole. Ann and I could barely stand to look at the stuff anymore, we were so sick of it! I felt as if I talked more in those few days at the Pole than I had in years, though it might just have seemed that way because Ann and I had talked so little during our trek. When we shook hands with some of the researchers after dinner and headed out to our tent, I could see that some of them felt sorry for us. They had no idea how happy I was to escape civilization and go back to the solace of my red tunnel tent!

chapter eight

TITAN DOME

The terrain Ann and Liv would head into for the second leg of the trip was new for both of them. Certain portions of their intended route had existed for thousands of years untouched by man. They would be the first expedition to descend the Shackleton Glacier. For both women, this second leg was the true milestone of the journey. Just setting foot on the other side of the Pole was in some ways a victory. For them, it was where they would be "explorers" in the truest sense of the word.

They would begin on the Titan Dome ice cap, the highest area of elevation on the continent apart from the Transantarctic Mountains. Buried underneath thousands of meters of ice (the base layer of which dates back 165,000 years) is a mountain range taller than the Appalachian Mountains of the eastern United States. The two would be climbing upwards of 11,000 feet (3,354 m). Because of the elevation, the air on Titan Dome would be thinner and colder than the air Ann and Liv had previously experienced. They would suffer shortness of breath, headaches, and fatigue from the altitude. Temperatures there would drop deep below zero. The coldest temperature ever recorded of −131°F (−91°C) was taken during the Antarctic winter at Vostok, a Russian research station east of Titan Dome. By comparison, at −58°F (−50°C), boiling water thrown into the air freezes instantly. At Vostok's record low, if a man were to go outside unprotected, his eyes would freeze immediately and within minutes the cold would penetrate his flesh and turn the muscle of his heart into a lump of ice. Ann and Liv would have their work cut out for them to save their fingers and toes while they traveled in the summer Antarctic temperature of "just" −35°F (−37.2°C).

The two would also be towing heavier sleds, re-stocked from their supplies at the Pole. It was no help that each of them had lost 20 pounds (9 kg) during the first half of the trip, likely due to their smaller rations near the Pole. Ann was down to 116 pounds (53 kg) and Liv was at 143 pounds (65 kg). They were hopeful that with full rations, they would regain their energy.

ANN

Liv and I left the South Pole on January 18. A crowd from the Pole gathered to see us off and get a glimpse of the sailing. Liv and I were nervous. Now that we had an audience, would we have wind? We were also worried about getting the sails tangled, which is pretty easy to do. Take-off is always the most precarious moment in that respect. The day was bright, and the sun glinted off tiny particles of ice in the air, making it shimmer. We had re-supplied from the cache of food and fuel we had shipped to the Pole, so our sleds were back at their original weight of 250 pounds (113 kg). They had weighed about 107 pounds (40 kg) by the time we made it to the Pole because we had consumed most of the food and fuel. That afternoon, the sleds seemed especially heavy as we waited for the wind to catch our sails. I held my breath, and then the slightest puff of wind came and lifted our blue NASA sails. As we pulled away from the dome, the people behind us whistled and cheered. I was very relieved.

Underneath my face mask, I could not stop smiling for an hour. I remembered how painful it had been in 1993 to watch another expedition that had flown in with us to Antarctica leave for the second half of their trek—the second half that we would not have a chance to attempt. I had watched them ski away down the runway, wanting more than anything to trade places with them. Now—eight years later—it was my turn. As Liv and I skied along, I noticed three clouds grouped together in the sky to the west. Seeing them made me think of my three mentors, all of whom have passed away. Pat

McCart, whose pouch I wore around my neck, was one. Another was a business woman in Minneapolis I met after my American Women's Expedition (AWE) trip. Her name was Linda Jadwin. Her company, Ceridian, threw a welcome home banquet for the expedition team when we returned to the Twin Cities. We had that huge debt to pay off, so it became a little fundraiser for us. From time to time over the next few years, it would get out in the news that I was still paying off my debt for that trip, and a few checks would come in. I always wrote personal thank-you notes, and I noticed that I was receiving a check from this woman at Ceridian regularly. I kept writing her thank-you notes, but by the time the fifth check or so came in, I wrote to her and said, "I want to meet you. I've never solicited you for a dime and these checks keep coming in. Your name is consistently at the bottom. I want to thank you in person to let you know how much this means to me." She wrote back and said that what she really wanted to do was to put together a luncheon and invite a group of women that she knew so they could meet me and ask questions. I agreed, and she put together the most interesting mix of people—businesswomen and artists and teachers and entrepreneurs—women who might not ordinarily have crossed paths. After that, Linda and I became personal friends, and she played a critical role in helping me make some choices about how to refocus the nonprofit foundation I had started for the AWE expedition. We turned it into a foundation that supports adolescent girls. More than anyone else I've ever known, she taught me the power of connecting people, especially women. She had a great talent for seeing the possibilities of collaborations, friendships, and partnerships. She knew how to fill a room with women who simply needed to meet each other. And she did it quietly, without any fanfare, supporting and elevating women by taking them into her circle.

The third mentor was my camp counselor from eighth grade, Kim Cook. Summer camp was always a place where I felt really good about myself. It was a formative experience that nurtured my love of the outdoors and sports. Kim had a way of making me feel included. During the school year, she would stop by the high school and round up a bunch of girls to play snow soccer. I was at the place in my life that most adolescents hit; you think your parents don't understand anything, and you don't fit in, and you have no clue where you're heading. And Kim just let me be me. I could hang around her and be this intense, overwrought high school kid, and she was always supportive. She's the one who encouraged me to keep a journal. When I look back, I am shocked that she made time for me and my dorky high school friends. We would bike two hours to the University of Minnesota so that we could hang out in her apartment. She was just a great refuge. I was devastated when she died in a car accident when I was a sophomore in college.

Seeing those three clouds together, I knew that wherever they were, my mentors were watching me and celebrating this moment. I giggled as I thought of all three amazing women, who had never met each other, getting to hang out. They really would have liked each other. And I really liked the idea of the three of them watching over me in Antarctica.

After sailing for 6 hours, we were both exhausted. Neither of us had rested well at the Pole, and our bodies were

struggling to adjust to the thirteen-hour time change. Technically, we had spent only one night at the Pole, but we lost an
extra day because we switched from Greenwich Mean Time
to New Zealand time (thirteen hours ahead), which is the
base's time zone; many flights to the South Pole originate
from New Zealand. We decided to switch back to GMT,
much to the relief of the team back at base camp as well. The
difference had meant that we were on almost opposite sched-
ules with Minneapolis and not awake at convenient times for
communication. With twenty-four hours of sun, we had the
luxury of adjusting our clocks to our bodies, instead of the
other way around.

LIV

On our second post-Pole day, we hit an area of deep, sticky
snow. It was like trying to ski on a sandy beach; the granules
of snow grabbed at the bottoms of our skis, making it impossible to glide easily. There was not enough wind to sail, just
enough to drive the cold through us. The temperatures had
dropped consistently to −35°F (−37.2°C). At that temperature,
moisture outside the body freezes instantly. Your breath forms
ice under your face mask. Your goggles frost inside and out.
When you exhale at night in the tent, your breath freezes on
the ceiling and then snows back down on you. We both wore
our down vests while pulling, something neither of us had
ever had to do before. Usually, the body heat we generated
when working so hard was enough to keep us warm. But
here, even with our down vests, we were cold. I had to work

to keep my fingers warm. Years ago, I had frostbitten the tips of the middle finger and the thumb of my right hand during my solo trek to the South Pole. I had made the mistake of cleaning ice from my goggles with a bare hand. The tips turned blue with frostbite; since then, they have been very sensitive to cold. It is much easier to get frostbite a second time, once the circulation is already damaged. Frequently during the breaks, I had to pump my arms like a windmill to get the circulation down to the hands.

For a spell, we were pulling long days in deep snow for little reward. I kept wondering whether we should continue. I worried that we would look foolish if we pulled for two weeks and then wound up calling for a pick-up because we couldn't complete the traverse in the remaining time. The prudent thing to do if we continued to have days with little progress would be to turn back, return to the Pole, and save the expense of a pick-up on the ice. I knew that this thought would not be a welcome idea with Ann. She had been planning this journey for years. Also, I knew it wouldn't go over well with the rest of the team. They would think we should press on as far as we could go.

Ann was so consumed with not letting her shoulder injury stop her that I didn't think she could consider whether it was wise to go forward in the first place. All her energy went into managing her pain. She is very stubborn and I respected her efforts; it was unbelievable in many ways that she had made it this far! Still, I was frustrated. Her persistence was driving both of us to pull the sleds for long hours. I had no problem keeping up with that. But the futility of it gnawed at me. These days of gaining three miles were like tears in a salty ocean. They would not amount to much.

But I realized that this was not my trip alone. It was not my decision only to make. There were other forces at play, as there always seem to be on expeditions. During those days, I was traveling in my head to other trips, remembering other hardships, as well as other victories. I revisited some of the crucial decisionmaking points in search of answers to my current dilemma. For some reason, I kept returning to my first unsuccessful attempt to cross Greenland. I was with three other women, and we had bad luck from the start. Less than a day into the journey, we were struck by what the Inuit call a *pitarq,* a storm of gravity-driven winds that hurl down a glacier with hurricane force. The wind was too strong to pitch a tent, so the four of us emptied all the contents of all four sledges into two of them and then lay back-to-back in the remaining empty two with tarp fabric over us. At one point when I thought the wind was easing, I wanted to secure the sledges with snow anchors. I raised myself up a little to listen. There was a violent roar, and I was lifted out of the sledge and flung onto my back. I couldn't see anything, just blinding white everywhere, and I had to fight my panic and the urge to sit up again. Cold and wet, I was able to raise up enough to see the red of the sledge tarps. I crawled the 10 meters (22 ft) back to the sledge and got back inside. We huddled in the sledges and waited out the storm for seventeen hours. And that was not to be our only challenge. While we were in the sledges, fuel had spilled into our food, contaminating it. A few days later, our Primus stoves stopped working—the company that had filled our order for fuel had sent *leaded* fuel, instead of the unleaded fuel we had requested. With little food and no stoves to melt ice to drink, we were in a pretty desperate situation. We activated our emergency beacon and made contact with an aircraft by radio. Within hours, new Primus stoves and a couple of hundred kilos of tinned food arrived by air drop. We also received orders to turn back immediately from the police in Godthaab, the administrative center of Greenland on the western coast. That order conflicted directly with the orders we'd received from the police in Angmagsalik on the eastern coast, who had told us to proceed no matter what: They did not have helicopters to rescue us. The four of us agreed that, with the airdrop, we were now in good condition and should continue westward.

A few days later, we were more than halfway across the glacier when an aircraft overhead radioed to us with a message from the police chief of Godthaab: "If you continue, your expedition permit will be withdrawn. In that case, your insurance, which is conditional on the permit, will be invalid." I was furious. He had no right to make that decision. Faced with a situation in which we would receive no help in the event of further trouble, we took a vote on whether or not to continue. I voted to press on, as did one other team member. But with half of the team ready to quit, we could not go on. We changed course and abandoned the expedition. We detoured to a hunting settlement nearby, where we were able to send our equipment home by boat. Later, I heard the story behind the ultimatum. The police chief had bragged at a local bar in Godthaalb that he would "get those females off the glacier." His decision had nothing to do with whether we were fit to continue. He was just angry because a group of women had defied him. A year later, I returned to Greenland with my friend Julie Maske, one of my partners from the failed expedition, and made the first successful, unsupported all-women's crossing.

I remembered how angry I had been when the decision to stop on that first trek had been made *for* me by the police chief. I knew that I couldn't do the same thing to Ann, even if I had better, legitimate reasons. Even if I could talk her into turning back, she would probably always wonder whether we had done the right thing, whether we could have made it— something I used to wonder often about during that first Greenland trip.

The police chief was not the first person to throw himself in the path to stop me, in part just because I was a woman. To some extent, the attitude persists in Norway that exploring or polar adventuring is a man's domain. I think that is wrapped up in the history of the country, which is filled with polar explorers: Norwegian Roald Amundsen was the first to the South Pole; and Fridtjof Nansen, the national hero who was intimately involved in negotiating the independence of Norway from Sweden, led the first expedition across Greenland. It is part of our lore and culture. For Norwegian children, learning to ski is as natural as learning to walk. But as the decades passed and women moved into many areas of life that men had once dominated (education, sport, business), polar exploration was one of the few remaining all-boys clubs. Some men still do not want to give it up.

When I first began skiing competitively as a young girl, there was still much resistance to women competing against men. The Birkebeinerrennet, a long crosscountry ski race of 34 miles (55 km) over a mountain range carrying a rucksack of 7.72 pounds (3.5 kg) was opened to women only in the late 1970s. I skied as a teenager in the first event in which women were allowed to participate, and I well remember the reaction of one of the old veterans when I overtook him on a downhill slope. He gave way, but whacked me over the neck with one of his ski poles and shouted, "Bloody woman!"

While I was pulling my sled on Titan Dome, I thought about how both Ann and I had spent big parts of our lives doing things that others said would be impossible. A good explorer challenges the limits of what is; and yet, a good explorer also knows when to quit—when the risks are too great or the efforts will be wasted. The line between tenacious and foolish is very thin. I was beginning to wonder whether we were erring on the side of foolishness. We still had more than 1,000 miles (1,609 km) to go, and less than a month to do it. I was not optimistic. But I could see there was a chance that I could be wrong. And as long as there was that chance—no matter how slim—I did not want to be the one to talk us out of moving forward. I decided not to share my thoughts of turning back with Ann.

ANN

A few days into the second leg, Liv was having a hard time with the pulling, I could tell. Not physically. Liv is tireless. She could pull me (and anyone else for that matter) into the ground. But emotionally, I could see her riding this roller coaster of expecting and anticipating wind, psyching herself up for it, and then it wouldn't come. We talked to John over the phone those first few days out of the South Pole chute, and his wind maps showed wind everywhere—except where we were. Pulling was tough, but mentally, I felt I was drawing strength from it. For me, the thing it takes to pull is my strength—stubbornness. All my life, despite my success at sports, I don't think I've ever been the biggest or the best at anything. I did well because I could outlast everyone. I was just too damn stubborn to quit. Pulling put me right back in that groove of slow and steady wins the race. I felt that I was in a contest against my sled, and at the end of the day when I unharnessed after six or nine hours of refusing to give in to pain or frustration or monotony, I would look back at the sled and imagine it sulking and beaten. I think part of what gives me that ability is that I try to stay in the moment and not get ahead of myself. For me, the pulling was a way to cope with the frustration of not having wind. What else could we do but sit in the tent and go crazy? Liv would wake up in the morning and get excited if the tent was stirring with a faint breeze. Then I'd watch her expression fall and her mood sink when the wind died. I chose not to follow her on those ups and downs.

For my part, I was dreading our next run of good sailing days. I wanted the wind to come so badly I could taste it. I knew we wouldn't finish this trip without it. Sure, I was getting better at the sailing; we both were. But I couldn't shake the feeling that up to that point I had been lucky. I was afraid my luck would run out.

We got our wind back on January 27. Although we had strong winds high up to pull our sails, the wind was also whipping up what's called a ground blizzard. It kicks up the loose snow on the ground into a cloud up to your waist or so. Above that level, you can see blue sky and have visibility for miles. Below it, you can't see your feet or the surface. The other nasty part of a ground blizzard is that it drives snow everywhere—down your pants, through the tent zippers, into your sleeping bag. Tent life gets tougher because you exert a lot more energy sweeping snow out of your clothes and you never really dry out. The snow you don't catch before your body heat melts it turns you into a damp, cold, shivering mess.

Ground blizzards are pretty dangerous to sail in, but we hung in there for seven hours of sailing and walking. The next day was pure sailing for seven and a half hours. We did the last two hours in one shot without stopping. That was a mistake. When we did stop, my right knee was in so much pain that I couldn't put any weight on it. I just sat down and groaned and cried. It took me a few minutes to recover. Liv seemed completely oblivious, tuned into some thought inside her head, focused on her sails. The weird thing was how quickly I felt fine. The intense pain quickly subsided once I moved around, and so I went to unpack my sail.

The wind was picking up so much that we decided to switch from the 15-meter sails to the storm sails. Liv went back to the sled to fetch hers, and I crawled back to get mine. First, the latch on my sail broke and it started to blow away.

Liv grabbed it just as it rolled between us. Then, while we were trying to untangle my storm sail, Liv let go of hers for a second. Zoom! There it went across the ice. I took off after it, huffing and puffing in the thin air. Not a sastrugi in sight for it to get hung up on! I caught up to it about a mile later, just as Liv sailed up behind me using her 15-meter.

Two days later, it was Liv's turn to go sail chasing. At about 8 P.M., I took a fall, no big deal. But as I was fumbling, being dragged, trying to pull the sail down, the metal latch that attached the sail to my steering bar snapped. I watched in horror as it just floated away from me. Liv was far ahead of me. I got up and pulled my Talkabout™ radio out and started yelling frantically on it to Liv, "Sail! Sail! Gone!" I could see her turn around and lock her gaze on the sail, now tumbling past her in yet another ground blizzard. She took off after it. I watched till I couldn't see her anymore. I walked up to her sled and waited. And waited. And waited. About twenty minutes passed. Ugly scenarios went through my head: What if she went too far away and got lost? I couldn't see any ski tracks to follow. I took the GPS position of the sleds and then started walking, following the wind into the direction it had carried the sail. After about three minutes of walking, I saw a figure in the distance, and as I got closer, I could see it was Liv—and she was holding something. I met her and took the wad of sail. She had lost her goggles and her face mask in the chase, so I gave her my glacier glasses.

That night in the tent we marveled at our adventure and our luck. As she warmed her ice-white fingers, Liv told me that Einar's note to her that morning had said, "No problem is so big that you cannot sail away from it." She shook her head, smiled and said, "I'm not sure how we are supposed to sail away from our problems when our sails want to sail away from us!"

We were in a good mood, for despite our sail trouble, the Transantarctic Mountains were growing on the horizon. That meant we would soon be sailing on Shackleton Glacier, which threaded between those mountains. The glacier was the gateway to the edge of the continent and the Ross Ice Shelf beyond it. The homestretch was in sight. More than 1,500 miles (2,414 km) down, just over 550 miles (885 km) to go. We had about twenty days left, which meant we needed to gain an average of 28 miles (44 km) per day. That didn't seem overwhelming when we thought about our last few days to the Pole. I was counting on a couple good days of 70-mile (112 km) gains to offset these slow, pulling stretches.

The first week of February did its best to beat the good cheer out of us. The ground blizzards continued. We were tent-bound twice that week because of a blizzard and poor visibility. The constant blowing snow found its way into our sleeping bags, our clothes, even our socks. I felt slimy and cold in my damp down suit. On the days when we were able to move, we found ourselves in a heavily crevassed area with a hard ice-pack surface. We had to punch along with our ski poles to test each step. The lighting was unlike anything I'd ever seen before. The swirl of snow blocked out most of the sun, creating a sense of dusk. It felt as though we were traveling at night. But then every once in a while a burst of sun would cut through the blizzard, almost like the sweep of a spotlight. It reminded me of those paintings where divine intervention is represented through the parting of the heavens by a bright burst of light. I was struck with wonder by the scenery. It was beautiful, exciting, eerie, scary—everything I had ever wanted in an expedition in this one place.

LIV

My sled was really starting to annoy me. It wandered left and right behind me, skimming over crevasses I had carefully avoided with my own steps. During a brief hour of sailing, it flipped over and a fuel bottle broke inside. The cold was intense, but bearable. To boost my spirits, I tried thinking about the wonderful trips I had taken with Einar on our ski tours on Arctic glaciers. By that day, Einar was already on his way to Tasmania. There, he would board the ship traveling to pick Ann and me up in McMurdo Sound. (Pam would fly to meet us in Tasmania on the way back.) Ann and I had about twenty days left to finish the Shackleton Glacier and the Ross Ice Shelf. Knowing that the boat soon would set sail—with Einar and Mariko Miyamoto, our champion in Cape Town, as well as a crew and numerous journalists—made our deadline more real. The ship, *Sir Hubert Wilkins,* was small for Antarctic waters, which were quickly freezing now at the end of the summer season. Each day that Ann and I pushed toward the Antarctic winter, we increased our own chances of encountering worse weather on land and of getting the ship stranded in pack ice. A sea rescue is not easy, nor is it cheap, to pull off. And the chance of injuries or deaths in the event of a storm or critical damage to the ship from pack ice was very real. I began to worry not only about what would happen to Ann and me but also what would happen to the people who were coming to meet us. I hoped that Antarctica would be kind— wind for us and steady seas for our loved ones.

Sporting our daily attire. Ann with "beak"; Liv with full mask and goggles, or, the "Darth Vader" look.

Happy to be here.

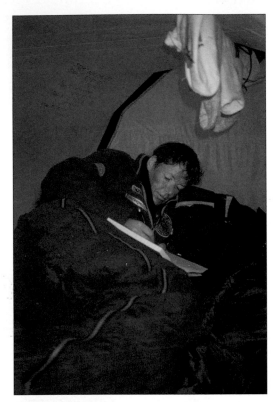

A typical evening: journal writing, laundry drying.

Hallelujah! Liv has spotted the other coast and the Transantarctic Mountains some 100 miles away.

Scouting for a way out of an icy, crevassed "Hell."

Though beautiful, the sun-cupped ice made skiing (and pulling) quite difficult.

Liv stops to make a regularly scheduled call to CNN.

Thinking light thoughts, Ann crosses just one of the hundreds of crevasses in our path.

Life on the "Shack": Endless pulling over rough terrain (above).
Portaging the Swithinbank moraine (below).

With Mount Speed, the last mountain on the Shackleton Glacier, in full view, and the Ross Ice Shelf in the distance, Liv reminded Ann that she had been trying for this moment for 11 years. Liv named it "Ann's day."

The end of the journey: ANI's small Twin Otter plane with skis picks us up on the Ross Ice Shelf.

Still friends on the other side. Deposited at the edge of the Ross Ice Shelf, we are ready to board the Sir Hubert Wilkins.

Reunions: Einar and Liv (left), Pam and Ann (below).

A view from and of the Sir Hubert Wilkins. *Antarctica is breathtakingly beautiful and alive with color but also a dangerous place for a ship to be at the end of the summer. It was time to go home.*

chapter nine

BEYOND ENDURANCE

ANN

Our first day on the Shackleton Glacier, February 6, was deceptively smooth. We sailed for the first bit down what was initially a gentle slope. The mountains rising on each side of us gave the place the feel of an enormous chute. This was why we had chosen to descend the Shackleton: We thought it would be faster and safer. But as we progressed, we found the combination of the strong wind, gravity, and the slick ice was carrying us way too fast to be in control. We would be sailing quickly and then suddenly wipe out painfully on the hard ice. Then we hit a crevassed area, and it was no longer safe to sail. Every third step or so, our ski poles broke through into deep fissures.

But the real nightmare began the next day. We would later name this place Hell. I'd never seen ice like that before; the whole glacier was a sprawl of ridges and crevasses. Imagine a dirt country road covered over with a thick layer of ice that dips and rises in the giant-sized potholes and tire treads. That was the Shack. Liv and I were like field mice trying to navigate that vast rutted mess. Much of the ice covering the crevasses was rotten (partially melted and crystallized). Despite our caution and testing with the ski poles, we both punched through the ice frequently. It's hard to explain what's going through your head when you fall through the ice up to your thighs or hips. First, there's the sensation of the ice crumbling beneath your feet and that rush of adrenaline as you feel yourself going down. At that point, you have no idea how deep the hole is. It could be that your foot will meet with solid ice a few feet down, one hopes with not enough force to break an ankle. But you could just as easily fall through to your elbows and find your legs dangling in the air above a crack in the ice that might go down for miles. You have a split second to catch yourself and try to stabilize on whatever edge of solid ice you can find. Then you have to worry about the sled. Sometimes, it can be your ally, helping suspend you and pull you out of the crevasse. But if the hole you fall into is downhill from your sled, it becomes a heavy torpedo rushing toward you, eager to crash through the ice and take you with it. Every time you punch through, your body reacts for the worst-case scenario, as if you had fallen into a bottomless pit. Your heart races, the adrenaline kicks in, and your body revs up with that survival instinct. What's more, you *expect* that fall with every step. The mental focus required is enormous, and the constant readiness is exhausting. The difference between dying in a crevasse and avoiding injury completely is a mix of experience, skill, reflexes, and luck. Liv and I stuck close together, within a few feet of each other, on this part of the Shackleton. More than once, we were able to help each other by holding each other's sleds out of crevasses or providing a hand to pull out of a hole. At the end of that first day, we were wiped out. We had traveled less than 11 miles (18 km) and spent more than nine hours pulling, mostly wearing crampons. The downhill slope of the glacier meant that with each step our toes were slamming into the fronts of our boots. We were sore and bruised when we made camp for the night. The gash in the side of Liv's sled was getting larger as it snagged the ice. It was impossible for her to control its path without her tow bar, and it would be pointless to repair it while we were still in this area of jagged ice.

Discouraged and tired that night, I called back to base camp. Stan Oleson picked up the phone. We chatted for a few minutes. He sounded pretty chipper, and about two minutes into our conversation about the ice, he told me why: He'd been waiting for a further analysis of a blood test that doctors thought initially showed signs of the return of the cancer—but that turned out not to be so. He was ecstatic, relieved. That made six months for him with a clean report. He'd kept the initial bad test result from us, thinking it would depress us on the ice. I was so glad to hear his news. I got off the phone and couldn't stop thinking about it. It put all the battles Liv and I were facing into perspective. I started thinking about conversations I'd had with Stan when I was in Minnesota, about how the cancer was affecting his life, how he was coping mentally and emotionally. One of the things he shared with me early on was that he had reached a kind of peace with the treatment process by *giving up* the fight against the cancer. Not that he quit trying to get well, but he had figured out that he couldn't spend his energy cursing the presence of the cancer in his life. It was useless to wonder "why me?" or to want things to be different. Once he accepted it as part of his life, he was able to put all his energy into getting well. He was even open to what he called the "blessings" of having cancer. He set up his radiation treatments during the day, and a different friend would come each day to pick him up and take him to the appointment. You could really see that feeling the warmth and support from his close-knit circle of friends was doing as much good for him emotionally as the radiation was doing for him physically.

Talking to him reminded me that I needed to let go of my anxiety about the wind, stop wishing for different weather, better ice, more time. Stan liked to compare the distinction he had learned to the difference between a Western saw and a Japanese saw: Western hand saws are designed to be pushed forward across the wood, a motion that strains your shoulder and puts tremendous pressure on the blade. By contrast, a Japanese saw is designed to be pulled across the wood as the arm draws in toward the body, a motion that applies more pressure to the wood by harnessing the natural circular motion of the shoulder. The saw cuts easily, in harmony with the body, so it is lighter and safer to use. I felt the resonance of that metaphor for the journey that Liv and I were on as well. It seemed to me that in this Hell, we had fallen into the mindset of fighting the ice. I wondered whether we could come up with a different way to approach it.

The next day, we decided to go forward moving one sled at a time together instead of pulling both individually. We moved one sled forward until we were just about to lose sight of the second sled and then parked it on a ridge where it would stay put. Then we went back and brought the other one forward. Although it seemed slower to move each sled independently, we saved a huge amount of time and energy we would otherwise have spent fishing our sleds out of crevasses. The next day, when the ice evened out a bit, we were able to hook the two sleds together, me pulling at the front and Liv braking from behind—our own version of a Japanese saw. We attached a 5-foot length of "webbing," a loosely woven flat rope, to the back of the second sled. Liv held that webbing, slowing our "sled train" when we were heading downhill and steering from behind around crevasses. We gained much more control and efficiency with this method of travel. But it did not make the terrain any less dangerous. And we were about to have a reminder of exactly how dangerous that part of the Shack was.

LIV

I still have nightmares about what happened on the Shackleton Glacier on February 9. To this day, it remains one of the most terrifying experiences I've had in all my travels. With the experience the two of us have, it should not have happened; but it's impossible to be 100 percent alert every second of the day. Yet even the slightest lapse in concentration can have terrible cost.

I was behind Ann, bending over to steer the back of her sled away from a crevasse. I had the webbing attached to the rear sled wrapped around my left hand. As I shifted my weight, I heard a warning crack, and in a split second, I had crashed through the ice up to my chest—into the very crevasse from which I had saved Ann's sled! There was nothing but air under my feet. I was dangling in a crevasse so deep that I could see it disappear into blackness meters and meters below me. I clenched the webbing, which had snagged on the edge of the crevasse in such a way that it was supporting me yet not transferring my weight to the sled. Without that tenuous anchor, the smooth-bottomed sled would have slipped just enough to send me falling. My right elbow rested on the edge of the hole. Quickly, I swung my right foot backward and planted it on the inside wall of the crevasse, digging my crampons in as deeply as I could. From there, I was able to lift myself into a swimming position over the crevasse and pull myself out. Meanwhile, the webbing had been holding the sleds behind Ann stationary. As I climbed out of the crevasse, the sleds jiggled and I heard Ann shout, "Don't push!"

My heart was pounding and I felt almost in shock from my own fear. I had no idea what she was so wound up about. I would find out later that she was warning me not to push the sleds from behind; had I shoved too forcefully getting out the crevasse, I would have pushed her forward into a crevasse in front of her. She hadn't seen me fall and had no idea what disaster we had narrowly avoided. The wind was too loud for her to have heard the crash of the ice. I couldn't see what was in front of her to be afraid of, either. We were both clueless. I thought sarcastically, "Gee, is this the thanks I get for saving her sled?" Suddenly, I just started laughing. The adrenaline rush had made me a bit punchy. I was grateful to be alive.

ANN

That night over dinner, I was horrified to hear from Liv how near we came to being in real trouble. I did not envy her close call, but the view from my end of the sled had not been too rosy, either. We would both be glad to be off the Shackleton soon.

Our last day on the Shackleton, February 10, we were finally able to get out of our crampons and put on skis. That was a huge relief. One of each of our crampons had broken while on the glacier. Our make-do repair job had made them even more uncomfortable—it was like walking in bad high heels at the end of a long day. We hadn't anticipated needing to use crampons as much as we did. If we had, we might have brought spares or rigged our boots differently. (The soft boots we had chosen to use because of their comfort for use with skis made for a lot of wear and tear on the crampons.) We didn't know when the ice would end, or whether our crampons would hold out long enough to cover it safely. That thought made me smile; I remembered the kind of shape Shackleton and his men had been in equipment-wise when the three-man party that went for help finally landed on the wrong side of South Georgia Island. Shackleton and his two men had then crossed a glacier to make it to a whaling camp on the other side of the island. They made makeshift crampons by extracting nails from their lifeboat and pounding them through the soles of their shoes. That they succeeded was nothing short of miraculous. By comparison, the tools we had on hand were luxurious.

In the late afternoon, we both surveyed the remaining field of glacier ahead of us. It was rocky snow, a white carpet flecked with giant chunks of pepper. To the right, the snow-capped mountains had big glaciers running down them. To the left, the rocks were a dramatic shade of red from mineral deposits. Despite our time pressure, we were enjoying this part of the trip. We took pictures of the spectacular scenery. We needed the beauty of this place to buoy our determination to continue.

But most of all, we needed to sail. We needed the miles. And we finally had a nice tailwind at our backs. The ice ahead was snow covered, but I knew the crevasses underneath would be wide, possibly big enough to swallow us, skis, sleds, sails, and all. But it did not look as bad as the terrain we'd just been through. I was scared. If Liv was, well, she didn't show it. I told Liv that I needed to think for a minute. I shuffled off a few yards away and looked out across the glacier and the ice shelf beyond. This was what it all came down to: eleven years of dreaming of going coast to coast. Was sailing here a reasonable risk, or would it be a reckless choice? We were at the wall for time. We needed at least a couple of days of 50-mile (80 km) gains to make it.

We decided to sail. It was wild. Liv took the lead with the 15-meter sail and I followed. I soon dropped back a bit because her sled was opening huge crevasses right in front of me. I had a few quick near-misses that got my heart thumping. We could see the translucent blue of the ice-covered crevasses as we approached them, and we both tried to ski across at an angle to minimize the time our weight was on thin ice. It was nerve-wracking. Liv dropped her sail after a few minutes and suggested that we switch to the storm sails. She was scared, and I didn't blame her. The storm sails were a little easier to control. We switched back to the 15-meter sails after a few miles, and Liv's got into a tangle on the way out of the bag. I told her to latch on to the back of my sled, and my 15-meter pulled us both through the deep snow for another seven miles or so! But the wind didn't last long. Both of us were cranky and irritable when we made camp that night. We hadn't gained many miles for all the hassle with the sailing, and we had created several hours of work for ourselves that night untangling lines and making repairs.

The next day, we both woke up in better moods, in part because the next milestone was within striking distance: the Ross Ice Shelf was less than 15 miles (24 km) away. The ice shelf is exactly what it sounds like: a huge floating mass of ice.

that spills off the edge of the continent. It is roughly the size of France, so it extends the apparent coast of the continent more than 400 miles (644 km) out to sea. The shelf was relatively flat, and from all we had heard, the wind really pounded down here. We anticipated being able to sail several long, full days. So as we pulled down out of the mouth of the glacier toward the shelf, I was feeling confident. It was our ninetieth day on the ice. With the prospect of gaining huge miles ahead of us, the time pressure receded. Both of us pulled and enjoyed the scenery around us. Mount Speed was to our left and the ridges of the Transantarctic Mountains rose behind us now. We pulled a little over 13 miles (21 km) in nine hours and camped at the foot of the Ross Ice Shelf.

I was so focused on the next day's sail and the beauty around me that the significance of our position hadn't sunk in. Liv turned to me once the tent was up, and said. "Hey, I think it is time for a little celebration, yeah? We have crossed the continent, Ms. Bancroft."

She was right! We were at the edge of the land mass! We had actually crossed the continent itself. In my mind, the remaining miles were definitely a part of the journey, but they were bonus miles when it came to setting history. We had just become the first two women to cross the land mass of Antarctica.

Liv filmed a little bit of me in front of the shelf, and we had our toast of Aquavit. It felt good, but still incomplete. To me, the expedition wasn't over, and it wouldn't be till we reached McMurdo station. That's the way we had planned it, and in polar expedition circles, I knew that a crossing without the shelf would not be considered official. In my mind, my childhood dream still had an asterisk next to it; I needed to cross the shelf to erase it. I knew we could do it. We were both in good shape physically and mentally; we had more than enough supplies. All we needed was a little wind.

LIV

Shortly after we made camp, I told Ann that we had to call this day "Ann's Day" because we had made it to the edge of the land. I had come up with that idea shortly after Titan Dome, when I had made peace with giving up the idea of turning back. I knew that it was not yet the perfect ending she wanted. But I forced us to celebrate it, to make note of it. I feared that we might have to be content with this mark as our success.

My note from Einar that day was *"Du må ingenting!"* "There is nothing you *have to* do." He was right. The expedition was of our choosing. It was good to be reminded that whether or not we went forward, it would be our own decision.

We had 489 miles (787 km) to go to McMurdo, and just ten days left. We needed a string of days that allowed us to travel as fast as we had on our best days, before the Pole. We needed that wind to return, and because we had not had it throughout the trip, I was afraid we were hoping for a miracle.

Unbeknownst to Ann and Liv, word of their historic first was already spreading around the world. Journalist Jerry Zgoda, who had been covering their trip for the *Minneapolis Star Tri-*

bune, was aboard the *Sir Hubert Wilkins* with Einar and Mariko. The ship received word from base camp that the two had made it to the shelf, and Zgoda filed a story by satellite. The headline for the Monday paper blared: "2 Women Conquer Continent." The article hailed the trip as the longest-known ski trek ever accomplished by women.

chapter ten

END OF THE JOURNEY

ANN

A breeze helped push us out of our cozy sleeping bags early on the morning of our ninety-first day on the ice. We started out with the 15-meter sails and sailed at a controlled pace through deep snow for half an hour. I was on autopilot. My arms and legs steered the sail and skis, but my brain refused to think about the miles remaining, or the odds against us. The wind died and we switched to pulling. I mechanically pushed each ski forward, feeling only the muscles of my thighs flexing and the weight of the sled pulling against my harness. For the first time in the journey, it was my heart that was numb. We pulled for nine hours. The wind kicked up from all directions throughout the day. It teased us into unpacking our sails, only to leave them lying limp on the snow and ice.

That night in the tent, I was tired beyond belief. We made a few media calls on a satellite phone that kept cutting out. Around midnight, I lay in the tent, trying to turn off my brain. I was overwhelmed with disappointment, but afraid to admit defeat. I wanted those last 400 miles (644 km) so desperately. If I forced myself not to make a decision about whether to continue, maybe our luck would break the next day.

The alarm went off at 6:30 A.M. the next morning, February 13. There was no wind. I reset the alarm for 7:30. At 8:30, I fired up the stove. I asked Liv about her nighttime thoughts about our time frame. Suddenly, I felt a huge, dry ball in my throat. There was no hiding my tears from Liv. For some reason, I was surprised by my reaction. I had known the time pressure existed and had thought about it on the glaciers, but only in general terms. I had avoided thinking through the specific consequences and how I would feel, in part because the only way I knew how to cope was just to plow ahead. If we didn't make substantial miles that day or the next, we were finished. Even then, we couldn't realistically make the miles we needed to before the deadline.

Liv and I decided to pull just to get out of the tent. We went for about seven hours, pointlessly barreling ahead. That night, we called Charlie, Stan, and John to talk about our options. They told us the decision was up to us. We asked for twenty minutes to think about it. I hung up the phone and

Liv and I looked at each other. Above us on the tent fabric, the black marker traced out the log of our trek—the last few entries of which would never be made. There really wasn't much to talk about. We knew all the reasons why we could not continue. The deadline for meeting our ship, *Sir Hubert Wilkins,* was nonnegotiable. To have a chance of making it out of McMurdo Sound safely, the *SHW* had to follow an ice breaker ship, one large enough and powerful enough to drive through pack ice. The last ice breaker would leave McMurdo Sound on February 23. So we had nine days left and 400 miles (644 km) left to McMurdo. We would need enough wind to travel 45 miles (72) each day. That was not impossible. But during the entire journey, we'd not had more than a four-day run of wind. There was no reason to think that we'd get that now. And if we just pulled along for eight miles a day, it would take us another fifty days to finish! We could send the ship back without us and fly out of McMurdo—if we were willing to spend enough money to cripple our young company and accept the ship as a wasted investment. But there would still be no way to be absolutely sure we could make it to the base on our own. The odds of a full-blown rescue were very good at this point because of weather. And it would be terribly irresponsible of us to jeopardize the Adventure Network International (ANI) pilots who would have to come and get us.

If Liv and I had been in it by ourselves, we probably would've gone a few more days before making the decision. But we had lots of other lives and investments to consider. It wasn't "my" or "her" trip, really. We had a responsibility to the people we'd involved—the kids, the base camp crew, our sponsors, ANI. Everyone was being super about letting it be our decision. But there was no question. I couldn't even get my denial to kick in, and I was working on overdrive to keep that in place. So we were very quick in making the decision. We used the minutes left to gain some composure. For me, it was like facing the sudden death of a loved one. I had to muster the composure to make the arrangements with a clear head. I placed the second call, but was barely able to croak out a hello before I choked up. I handed the phone to Liv.

LIV

Charlie immediately made me smile by teasing, "So, how many miles have you made since we last spoke?" I laughed because it was a way to not cry. Really, I think still if the wind had started at that moment, we both would have hung up and raised our sails. We were so bitterly disappointed. But we knew the right thing to do.

"So." Charlie hesitated; then, "What are you two thinking?"

"Well, we see the writing on the wall," I said simply. "We agree we should call for a pickup."

That was that. Charlie and Stan talked with us for a few minutes about logistics: whether we could change our minds once the call was made; how long it would take a plane to reach us. Charlie was adamant that the team had to agree before he called ANI. He suggested that if Ann and I made significant progress the next day, around 62 miles (100 km), then we would put off the decision one more day. But the next time we had one more windless day, the expedition would be over. Ann and I agreed.

⌒ ⌒ ⌒

The next day, February 14, at 3:00 A.M. Central Standard Time (10 A.M. on the ice), the phone rang in John Tuttle's empty office. Voicemail picked up. In a thick voice, Ann recorded a message: "Hi, Charlie, Stan, and John. Ann and Liv here. If you've checked in with our Argos position, you probably know what I'm about to say. There is no wind. And so we didn't get our sailing day to keep this thing alive one more day. Feel free to do what you need to do with ANI and get the information to get that process moving."

Later that day, the base camp team talked with Ann and Liv to plan the pickup. Ann and Liv were despondent. Both were mourning the last lost miles and a journey that to both of them, as expeditioners, would always be incomplete. Although on some level, Charlie and the rest of the team understood Ann and Liv's distress, they considered the trip an overwhelming success. The media had heralded Ann and Liv's crossing of the Antarctic land mass as a historic first. More than 3 million kids in 116 countries had followed their trek via the Web site. The reach of the trip was undeniable. But huddled in their tent at the bottom of the world, Ann and Liv did not yet see it.

Charlie struggled for words to comfort them. "From the public's perspective, from the perspective of the school kids, your dream of crossing the continent has totally been realized.

People get that. You made history. They're all looking at this part, the ice shelf, as getting off the continent, as opposed to finishing the expedition."

After a long pause, Stan added, "Though that may not be the way you look at it."

"No, it's not," Liv said. "This is just really emotional for Ann and for me, too. But we do understand what you're saying, Charlie, about the reaction. We're happy that people feel that way."

Afraid that Liv might be backpedaling, Charlie started to make the team's case for stopping. "I don't think that we would have made this recommendation if we didn't think safety has to be the number-one priority. . . . It's difficult . . ."

"Charlie," Liv cut him off. "We totally agree with you. This is the right decision. And when we see that people around the world got our message about dreams, we understand that. But we are just (her voice breaks) . . . personally disappointed."

The mood around the conference table was somber as the team wrapped up the conversation. Stan would get back to Ann and Liv with instructions from ANI for marking out a runway. Charlie passed on more times for media interviews. And then Zoë Alderfer Ryan popped her head into the conference room with a question: "Hey, do you want to talk to a school?" Several previous attempts to connect Ann and Liv with classrooms while on the ice had fallen through due to spotty connections or bad weather. Ann and Liv dutifully agreed to take the call, which was then tacked onto their schedule after an interview with CNN. Zoë had picked a classroom of fourth- and fifth-graders in Fairibault, Minnesota. The class had been following Ann and Liv's journey and writing stories about the trek for their local newspaper. Ann and Liv were less than eager to make the call, figuring they would have a roomful of disappointed children to console while feeling so low themselves. The next day, they set aside their departure preparations to make the call. Ann steeled herself, and then dialed.

In a cramped classroom on the other side of the globe, seventy-eight kids were crowded around a telephone, which sat on a stool in the middle of the carpeted floor. As the phone rang, several children gasped audibly and covered their mouths, eyes wide open with shock. They couldn't believe it. Ann and Liv were calling *them* from Antarctica! Teacher Sarah Juncker answered the call. Ann and Liv could hear the children scuffling closer to the speaker phone as the teacher greeted them. Tearfully, Juncker thanked the two explorers for allowing the kids to be part of their journey. She said they couldn't know how important their lessons had been to the kids. Then it was the children's turn to speak. One by one, kids knelt next to the phone and read the questions they had prepared on index cards: How does it feel to be the first two ladies to cross Antarctica? How did it feel when you went looking for sponsors and they told you that you were too small? How did you meet each other?

Ann and Liv, sitting cross-legged in their tent with their ears pressed to the phone held between them, answered the questions, warming to the kids as the call went on. The kids sang a song they had written for the two about fixing their sails with dental floss. After a few more questions, a small, dark-haired boy approached the phone and identified himself as Logan. He carried an index card, but he didn't refer to it. He leaned over the phone and simply said, "I just wanted to tell you that both of you have been real role models to me. Sometimes I have a hard time with school, and I just used to feel like there were lots of things that I could never do. And now that you guys have done this, I see that I can do anything I put my mind to. You changed my life."

In the pause that followed, Ann and Liv's disappointment and fatigue fell away. Suddenly every fall, every mile, every injury, each bowl of oatmeal choked down, seemed worth it— for Logan and the others out there just like him.

For the first time in many days, Ann and Liv smiled.

ANN

That phone call changed our world. I'll never forget the little boy who talked about his own struggles. He's the one who undid me. I could just tell that this was the first time he was ever sharing beyond his teacher his troubles in school and what it meant to follow us. What struck me was that he was so articulate in drawing the lines, the threads between what we were doing in following our dream and what he wanted to do and the struggles he was having in achieving his goals. That's in essence what we wanted to have happen. And so we were drawing strength from these little fifth graders who really, in my mind, were telling us that we had achieved the purpose of our journey, the bigger journey.

What we heard in that phone call was the whole reason for the trip. It was the tonic I needed. We talked almost forty minutes with the kids, which was unheard of for us. We just didn't want the call to end.

LIV

The whole time during the call and hearing these children from Fairibault, I was thinking about Ann. I was remembering the stories she had told me about Pat McCart, the teacher who showed Ann her own talents; the high school guidance counselor who helped her get a last chance to pass her teaching test; people who had intervened and changed her life, created that pivotal moment for her. And there we were, witnessing how our trip had done the same for these children. It was too much happiness to hold. We had spent years planning and dreaming about the perfect crossing. But we had spent our whole lives hoping that others would be inspired by our passion, hoping to pass on what our teachers and mentors had given us. In that, we had succeeded. In that light, 400 miles was not important.

⌒〜　　　⌒〜　　　⌒〜

The next day, Charlie shared over the satellite phone an editorial from the pages of the *Minneapolis Star Tribune*. It read in part:

> Some of us, had we just finished skiing across the Antarctic continent, might call it quits on reaching the

Ross Ice Shelf. Park that 250-lb sled, step out of the harness, call for an air taxi to McMurdo. Kick back with hot coffee and a little Aquavit.

Really, who needs the extra points after a 90-day traverse of mountains, glaciers, and crevasses? Who would be up for skiing another 500 miles across a floating pad of sea ice, racing against the clock to reach open water before the ship for home must sail?

Ann Bancroft is up for it, and so is Liv Arnesen. And if you aren't up for cheering them on, if the next week seems a bit anticlimactic to you, perhaps you miss the point of their effort.

The Bancroft Arnesen Expedition isn't about spots on a map, or historic firsts, or even about proving women's capability. It's about realizing personal dreams, as the trekkers point out at every opportunity, and about honoring a portion of the human spirit that can be outlined, if only vaguely, with words like devotion, self-reliance, endurance . . . In the end, the forces that pull people to the ends of the earth, that push them to their limits and beyond, are intensely personal. They motivate an interior exploration that, it often seems, has pauses, but no endpoints, and lies somewhere beyond the explorer's capacity for description. Such inquiry is striking in an era when so many surveys of the soul seem to follow the same well-trod tracks, like a credit-card vacationer.

This point eludes the carpers who deride descriptions of Bancroft and Arnesen as explorers. Like all the rest of the world, they note, Antarctica has already been explored; moreover, we live in a time when crossing Greenland, climbing Everest, circling the globe by hot-air balloon are becoming mere pastimes for the super-rich.

Yes, but out on the Ross Ice Shelf today are two ex-schoolteachers in their middle 40s who found the inner and outer resources to ski 2,300 miles across the world's most difficult landscape, dragging their gear. If "explorer" is too lofty, call them adventurers, expeditioners—or best of all, heroes.

chapter eleven

A NARROW ESCAPE

ANN

Getting picked up off the ice shelf was a delicate production. We had to wait several days for weather with good visibility, both at our location on the shelf and at Patriot Hills on the other side of the continent where Adventure Network International's (ANI) plane would take off. That late in the season, the weather was changing almost every fifteen minutes, which reinforced the urgency of getting off the shelf soon. Winter had clearly arrived. We had trouble getting enough juice in our satellite phones to discuss the landing with ANI. (We had run down our battery with the call to the kids in Fairibault, and after that we had sparse sunshine to charge our solar panel.) On the afternoon of February 16, ANI let us know that the small propeller plane on skis that would pick us up had left Patriot Hills.

We figured we had plenty of time; the flight from Patriot Hills would take eight hours. We had already pulled to the flattest spot we could find, which, to be honest, was not very flat. The whole area was riddled with sastrugi, depressing evidence of the typically constant winds on the shelf. So we piddled around trying to charge the satellite phone, packed our things, and ate some lunch. Our batteries were all worn down, so we were carrying them around in our shirts, trying to eke that last bit of juice out of them by keeping them warm. Eventually, according to ANI's instructions, we used our gear to mark off a runway. We took our brightly colored food sacks and dropped them every 100 yards (91 m) or so, weighted down or staked down to prevent them from blowing away. We weren't exactly sure how safe the runway was—there was no way to know whether there were crevasses hidden under the icy path we'd chosen. Within minutes of laying the runway, we heard the faint buzz of a plane overhead. Then we could see it. It was obviously flying toward McMurdo, but it was way too high in the sky to be looking for us.

Liv, who was inside the tent, called out, "Is that them?" I looked up and said, "I don't think so." She yelled from the tent, *"Who else could it possibly be?"* She was right. They just hadn't seen us! I could finally spot them, a tiny speck high above us. They were not even looking. They'd obviously been circling lower somewhere else and were on their way to McMurdo.

Liv started throwing stuff out of the tent at me—fuel bottles and anything she thought I could light. So I was out there burning granola, sports drink powder, anything we had to send some smoke into the air that the plane might see. Then, miraculously, the plane turned around—not because of our little pyrotechnics show; they had spotted the red tent. It was complete luck. The weather and visibility were pretty bad, and the only reason they were in the air was that they didn't expect conditions to get any better. The season had turned on a dime. On the first pass, they couldn't see us and had given up and decided to fly on to McMurdo. But there was a third guy from ANI in the back of the plane, and he saw the red dot of our tent.

The pilot touched down carefully along our runway, stopping just short of the tent. The weather closed in right behind him with a virtual whiteout. The crew got out of the plane, said hello, and informed us that there was no way we were getting off the shelf that day. Then they started pitching a tent. When Liv and I went out to collect our gear from the makeshift runway, we discovered that while landing, the plane had opened up a huge hole—easily big enough to swallow a passenger bus. We had laid the runway over one of the largest crevasses Liv and I had seen on the trip. Once the three men had pitched their tent, we told them about the hole, so they took shovels and probing sticks to try to find a better runway for when we would need to take off. They wound up finding several more large crevasses. The shelf was full of them!

We waited for two days for the weather to clear at McMurdo and on the shelf. In the meantime, the pilot started to talk about how the weather was better over at Patriot Hills, and it might be easier to just fly there instead. Liv and I were panicked. That would mean missing the boat at McMurdo and ruining the reunion with the team, not to mention adding the cost of flying back from Patriot Hills to Chile, or wherever else ANI decided to drop us off!

With the teeny amount of battery power left in the phone, I called Charlie to warn him. I was worried that the pilot might be using the weather as an excuse to do what was easier for him—return to base. I had no authority to challenge him, and I certainly didn't want him to make a risky decision. At the same time, I had no idea whether he was telling the truth, given our experience with ANI. I wanted him to challenge the weather prudently to get us where we were supposed to go.

As soon as Charlie picked up the phone, I said, "Charlie, don't talk. Just listen. Do whatever you can on your end to pull strings and keep pressure on ANI operations that we need to go to McMurdo, because they're starting to talk about a different site. And we can't argue with a pilot who says, 'This is your option,' because we can't argue about weather and safety." I barely had those words out of my mouth before the phone went dead. We would just have to hope that Charlie had heard and understood me.

LIV

On February 18, we awoke in the middle of the night to the sound of fuel drums rolling across the ice. The two of us sat up and put our heads out of the tent. The ANI group was all packed and ready to go. Ann and I were thinking, "Gee, were you going to wake us?" We quickly gathered our sleds and took down the tent. The crew asked us to stand at the edges of the original runway we had marked out, figuring that the plane already had opened the only crevasse in that path. To try a new one would risk more unknown surface. The plane started and rumbled slowly past Ann and me to the end of the runway, just short of the big crevasse. Then it turned around. We ran to the plane and jumped on board. In a few seconds, we were up and off into the sky. I looked out of the window for a last look at the shelf we had not covered, but it was hidden by the swirling snow.

ANN

For all my distrust of ANI, I cannot blame the pilot for not wanting to land at McMurdo, an American research base. The place is famous for its unwelcoming, almost hostile, attitude toward visitors. Our troubles began before we even landed. The tower at McMurdo wasn't being overly forthcoming about weather conditions. We were trying to land a plane on a sheet of ice, and the bureaucrats below were worried about breaking their policy by "assisting" us. The pilot, a Canadian, joked that it was good we had at least one American on board—me—so they would be less likely to shoot us out of the sky! I was embarrassed by my country's poor hospitality. The South Pole has mellowed because it is a destination, and the folks there seem to find an easier way to walk the line between providing undue assistance and being friendly. For McMurdo, visitors are rare. It was much more uptight about our presence. The station has strict protocols about how the personnel can interact with expeditioners such as Liv and myself, or, as the McMurdo bureaucrats would describe us, "glorified tourists." Many years ago, when a commercial plane crashed into nearby Mt. Erebus, McMurdo was criticized for its response to the accident. That was the beginning of a groundswell of opposition to anyone except researchers having access to the continent. The base's response to the criticism was to attempt to wash its hands completely of association with treks such as mine and Liv's. The McMurdo top brass would have preferred that we weren't there at all, and they had made plenty of rules to ensure that we knew that. We felt ill at ease as our little plane touched down, especially once we heard that, although the mini-helicopter from the *SHW* that would fly us to the ship deck had arrived at the base, the weather had closed in. We would have to spend the night at McMurdo.

McMurdo is enormous, known as "the city" on Antarctica. We never even saw McMurdo proper while we were there. We were kept on the outskirts of "Mac Town," as it is known, out by the airstrip and some off-site buildings. As we taxied in, the tower told us where to park. The pilot maneuvered the plane to the designated space. He turned off the engines and we prepared to exit the plane. Suddenly, we noticed that we had been followed by a white van, which stopped a short distance in front of the plane. The passenger window rolled down and a camera lens poked out and started taking pictures of us. We were under surveillance! I was completely embarrassed by the rude reception, and none of us knew exactly what to do. Could we get out of the plane? There was a crowd of people in red jackets on the other side of the runway, all staring at us, nobody making a move toward the plane. Meanwhile, the van's engine was running and that camera was still trained on us. Finally, the pilot took charge. He hopped out of the plane and walked over to the van to talk to someone inside. He confirmed that we were in the right spot and got permission to pitch his tent under the wing of the plane. As he walked back toward us, the van drove away.

Liv and I got out and starting unloading our gear. It was super cold. All the time, the group of people in the red jackets were staring at us. Liv and I didn't know what to do. We were feeling a little shy, and we didn't want to get anyone into trouble. And we weren't entirely clear about whether the crowd was friendly or not. But as the white van disappeared from sight, the people started to wave, and a few of them started jumping up and down and calling to us. These were our fans at McMurdo. They had been following us for the entire trek. But it turned out that McMurdo policy forbade them to come onto the runway and talk to us! We had to go to them. Still not quite understanding why they were frozen in place, Liv and I sheepishly walked over and said hello. We were immediately enveloped in their warm welcome. One of my expedition partners from the American Women's Expedition (AWE), Anne Dal Vera, had spent the summer at McMurdo running the waste recycling program. She had told her friends all about Liv and me and had whipped up the station's interest in us. In fact, we had just missed Anne. She had flown out that morning. (At that point in the season, McMurdo was in the process of sending almost all its people off the continent before the winter arrived.)

The people in their red National Science Foundation (NSF) parkas took us to a little galley there off the airstrip. The cook came out, put on his apron, and offered to sneak us some food. The staff had all brought treats they'd been saving—brownies and beer, things from their family care packages, a bucket of fruit. At some point, someone showed up with fresh towels, so we took sponge baths in the restrooms there. People came visiting all night long. They had wind of our arrival up in Mac Town, and found ways to get car rides down to us. They actually woke up someone to open the post office so we could buy stamps for our letters and postcards. So despite the official cold shoulder, we felt well cared for.

LIV

About mid-afternoon of the next day the helicopter pilot let us know we had a window of good weather. We said our good-byes to everyone, as if we had known them for weeks. When I reached the landing pad, I was shocked by how small the helicopter was. It looked like a toy helicopter, with barely enough room for two! I got in next to the pilot, and then Ann got in. She couldn't even shut the door properly—there was a

gap of sky peeking between the door and the side of the helicopter. So I stretched my arm over Ann's shoulder and
grabbed the handle of the door so she would not fall out. The
pilot asked if we wanted to do some sightseeing from the sky.
I immediately said, "No!" I knew people who had been killed
in toy helicopters such as this one. Ann was more polite and
pointed out a mountain ahead of us. I was thinking at that
point that I would have felt safer in a giant cargo plane filled
with fuel drums and Russian smokers!

We flew for about ten minutes before I saw the ship. It
was tiny as well. As the helicopter circled the boat to land, we
could see flags running in a line from the mast to the bow:
Norwegian, American, Australian, South-African—every one
you could imagine. I saw people on deck and recognized
Mariko, Michael, and Einar! He was not hard to spot—tow-
ering over everyone in his orange down jacket and funny hat.
I smiled and got this good, warm feeling inside. The helicopter landed on the ship's deck pad and we spilled out. I noticed
that people stepped back for Einar and me to meet, and I felt
suddenly self-conscious about our public reunion. But in a
second he was cupping my face in his hands, laughing, kissing,
and crying, saying nothing at all.

We went inside, and there was a spread of food and wine,
all the luxuries we had forgone for the trip. Everyone was trying to be respectful and quiet, keeping in mind that we had
been in isolation for so long. Seeing this many people all wanting to talk to us at once was overwhelming. Then, Mariko gave
us the good news: We had received permissions to visit both
Shackleton's and Scott's huts! Ever since I was a girl, I had

stared at the pictures of the huts that both Shackleton and Scott had lived in on the Antarctic coast with wonder—would I ever get to see them? Now that lifelong desire was coming true.

ANN

Visiting Shackleton's hut at Cape Royds was the perfect ending to our trek. It was like coming full circle. We had a chance to walk into the very pictures we had pored over as girls dreaming of Antarctica. Shackleton was a thirty-four-year-old lieutenant in the British Royal Navy when he built the hut in 1908. It became the base of operations for his second Antarctic expedition, in which he tried to be the first explorer to make the South Pole. That expedition, like the later *Endurance* quest, ultimately failed. Again, Shackleton proved wise and judicious, making a tough decision that saved lives. Recognizing that they did not have enough provisions to make the pole and the return trip, Shackleton turned his men back just 97 miles (156.10 km) from the South Pole. Just 97 miles! Fresh from making my own prudent but difficult decision, I felt a new level of kinship with my hero.

Shackleton's hut is like a museum, perfectly preserved just as he left it. Cannisters of cocoa and food sit on the shelves, along with shards of pottery. There's a black double-oven stove, pans still sitting on the long-cooled burners. In the kitchen area, big boxes labeled "British Antarctic Expedition 1908" are stacked almost to the ceiling. A row of boots and shoes are lined up near the stove, probably placed there at one point to dry out. And Shackleton's desk, a slab of wood across two packing crates. From reading about it and seeing pictures, I knew the angles of that entire hut by heart. In some ways, it was like visiting my grandmother's house or someplace just as familiar.

We sailed farther down the coast to Cape Evans, where the hut that Scott built on his fatal trek for the South Pole stands. In Scott's hut, you can almost hear the voices. It appears that they left in a hurry; there's a mess of dishes and clothes strewn about inside. Liv and I both took turns sitting at Scott's desk. Outside is a petrified dog corpse, its collar still on, and rounded bales of hay for the expedition's ponies dot the space between the hut and the stable. You can actually still smell the hay.

These shacks were the history that had motivated our journey. These were the men whose lives had stirred our imagination. I thought about Shackleton and Scott almost every day of the trek—sometimes in relationship to how they had endured worse conditions, sometimes just feeling reverence for them. I felt a sense of camaraderie, both because of the long relationship I'd had with them and their stories as well as the ironic intimacy of Antarctica: So few of us have been to its vast interior. But I didn't feel that I belonged there, or that I had joined their club. These guys were in a totally different league.

LIV

Walking around in the huts felt unreal to me. I felt as though I had been sent back in time or dropped into the pages of one of my well-worn childhood books. We had spent hardly a few minutes on the ship before leaving for the huts. My thoughts were still scattered and I was trying to process it all—that the trip was over, that these other people around me were real, that I was standing in the birthplace of my dream. No one spoke, as though we were all trespassers on sacred ground. Inside Shackleton's hut, I felt similar to the way I had eight years earlier on Christmas Eve when I had reached the South Pole on my solo trek. I was drained and empty. Inside my heart, the place where my ambition to cross Antarctica had dwelled, was now vacant. But I did not feel the same contentedness that I had years ago on my solo trip. The fact that the ice conditions had forced us to fly over the last part of the shelf did not feel good. Ann, our team, and I had planned this expedition for two years; Ann and I had labored 97 days on the ice. Now it was over. What now? My thoughts flew to Shackleton. He was a happy man—as long as he had a project to plan or was on an expedition. His happiness depended so much on those things that he became obsessed, and that obsession with Antarctica led to his death. What about me? Would the disappointment of not skiing all the way to McMurdo fade? Or would it haunt my dreams and drive me to come try once more?

As we walked away from Shackleton's hut and down to our ship I felt I knew the answer. I would not wind up as the explorer who had built this hut. I would be able to let go of my dream, having given it all of my effort and energy and will. It was over. Time to let go. Time for a new dream to take up residence in my heart.

The ship sailed the short path to Cape Evans and Scott's hut next. The crazy wastefulness of building two similar huts so close together on Antarctica is a testament to the hatred and competition between these two English explorers. In 1902, Scott made his first attempt to reach the South Pole and Shackleton was part of his team. The two butted heads often on the failed expedition and parted as enemies. Six years later when Shackleton returned as the leader of his own pole-bound expedition, Scott refused to let Shackleton use his precious hut. So Shackleton built his own. I thought of some of the fateful decisions Shackleton made on that trip. He had sailed to Antarctica via The Bay of Whales. Just three years later, Roald Amundsen made his camp at the mouth of that bay in part because that starting point shortened the distance to the pole. Had Shackleton made his camp off The Bay of Whales instead of here, his journey likely would have succeeded, and we Norwegians would have one less hero. The passing of time and hindsight give new contexts to decisions. I wondered if someday I would feel more content around our decision to end the journey when we did, or if the "what ifs" would continue. My own life, for instance, might have turned out very differently, had Shackleton discovered the pole. I might never have known much at all about this frozen place at the bottom of the world, let alone be tied to it through my lifelong dreams.

As we walked from our ship to Scott's hut, I remembered the difficult period I had hit on Titan Dome, before I was completely committed to not turning back. My thoughts had drifted to Scott and his men frequently. They had suffered so desperately from scurvy, frostbite, and gangrene. It made me realize how lucky Ann and I were, even in what was for me a difficult moment. What was time pressure compared with the risk of losing health and life?

We walked quietly into Scott's hut, as if we were a little afraid we would disturb someone inside. Indeed, it looked as though the explorers might return any minute. Clothing and dishes were strewn about. I felt as though I had entered someon's private cabin without permission and I was relieved to leave and climb to the memorial site overlooking the hut.

Outside, Ann and I called Charlie on the satellite phone. We had shared so many of our sad moments over the last few days with him. It seemed only right to share our elation at being in this historic place. He sounded happy, more upbeat, more like the Charlie we knew. I'm sure he recognized a more positive note in our voices as well.

⌣ ⌣ ⌣

The arrival at the boat was the beginning of a challenging two-week-long chaotic and stormy trip during which everyone except Ann was constantly seasick. Instead of a flight, Ann and Liv had chosen the slow boat journey away from McMurdo to Hobart, Tasmania, in part to gain a gentler re-introduction to civilization; Ann and Liv had been in solitude in Antarctica for ninety-seven days. Ann had a teary reunion with Pam in Hobart, where both couples stayed two days together. Then the two couples flew to New York so that Ann and Liv could give a round of media interviews.

Even as Ann and Liv emerged from their Antarctic cocoon, they were only dimly aware of the far-reaching impact of their journey. Back in New York, after they were interviewed by David Letterman and Katie Couric, the two were stopped on the street by strangers and asked for autographs. (Atwood noted with considerable satisfaction that the two made all their appearances dressed in their polar fleece gear, not in skimpy dresses.) When Ann returned to Minneapolis, she marveled at how the letters and printed-out e-mails from their supporters nearly filled Liv's training sled.

As a whimsical gesture while still on the ship, Ann and Liv took a soda bottle and crammed inside it a plastic logo from the expedition and a note from the two of them to the person who discovered the bottle. The act is a tradition at the end of expeditions, a sort of a symbolic statement announcing to fate and the world, "I was here." But for Ann and Liv, their impact was far from just symbolic. Millions of people had already been touched by their trip. All told, over 3 million school children from five continents had followed the trip via *yourexpedition*'s online education partnerships. *Yourexpedition* received (and responded to) more than 20,000 letters and e-mails sent to the two women; the messages told stories about how Ann and Liv had inspired people, young and old, to pursue their dreams. And the two women, as well as their team, were irrevocably changed.

ANN

I don't know how the history books will choose to record the Bancroft-Arnesen Expedition. We accomplished several firsts for women—the first crossing of the land mass; the longest ski expedition ever for women. But within expedition circles, the trek will never be considered "crossing the continent" without the Ross Ice Shelf. I still have trouble with that. I think we made the right decision and that comforts me. But I don't feel vindicated. I'm proud that we had the ability to make that decision, but it still stings. I think it's fitting that, in the end, the very children we had sought to inspire and to teach wound up being the ones to remind us of our own lesson: the joy is in the journey. More important than the specific dreams you dream is the reason *why* you dream—and that reason is for the experience of *living the dream,* not for the accolade of having achieved it.

People have run through the "what ifs" with me: What if we had taken the shorter, more traditional route across the continent? What if we had not been delayed in Cape Town? What if we had chosen Punta Arenas as a departure point instead? Any one of those changes might have made a difference. But when I think about the expedition, that's not what I think about. I remember the sound of Liv's laugh and the snow crunching under my skis, the majesty of the Wolf's Tooth, the splendor of the sastrugi. Why? Because even if I had a guarantee that one of those factors would have allowed us to cross the shelf, I still wouldn't change a thing. Honestly. That was something I figured out on the voyage to Hobart. I kept coming back to two pages in the book that Pam made for me to carry across the ice. They were an excerpt from the book *Kitchen Table Wisdom: Stories That Heal* by Rachel Naomi Remen, M.D. The selection was from my friend, Alice Johnson, who (of course) couldn't follow the rules and pick a poem. The book chronicled Remen's work with AIDS/HIV patients and what she had learned from them about living with a reality that is different from the illusory, perfect one we would imagine:

. . . I had thought joy to be rather synonymous with happiness, but it seems now to be far less vulnerable than happiness. Joy seems to be a part of an unconditional wish to live, not holding back because life may not meet our preferences and expectations. Joy seems to be a function of the willingness to accept the whole, and to show up to meet with whatever is there. It has a kind of invincibility that attachment to any particular outcome would deny us. Rather than the warrior who fights toward a specific outcome and therefore is haunted by the specter of failure and disappointment, it is the lover drunk with the opportunity to love despite the possibility of loss, the player for whom playing has become more important than winning or losing.

The willingness to win or lose moves us out of an adversarial relationship to life and into a powerful kind of openness. From such a position, we can make a greater commitment to life. Not only pleasant life, comfortable life, or our idea of life, but all life. Joy seems more closely related to aliveness than to happiness. . . .

Later, Remen writes:

There is a fundamental paradox here. The less we are attached to life, the more alive we can become. The less we have preferences about life, the more deeply we can experience and participate in life. This is not to say that I don't prefer raisin toast to blueberry muffins. It is to say that I don't prefer raisin toast so much that I am unwilling to get out of bed unless I can have raisin toast, or that the absence of raisin toast ruins the whole day. Embracing life may be about more than tasting whether it is either raisin toast or blueberry muffins. More about trusting one's ability to take joy in the newness of the day and what it may bring. More about adventure than having your own way.

I like what that passage says about where to look for joy. I think she's right. The real joy for me in the expedition was the expedition itself: The kids I met, the places I saw, the things I learned. What's more, I would go one more step and argue that sometimes the outcome that you become attached to *isn't* the best scenario. Ultimately, I think the kids following our trek learned more than they would have had we crossed the shelf without a hitch. They were exposed to an entire conversation that otherwise would not have happened about tough choices and responsibility and the point of dreams. And because the biggest reason for the expedition was to touch kids' lives, that was the better outcome. I guess what I mean is this: No matter what past experience has taught you, no matter what you *think* you want, sometimes the blueberry muffin *is* better than the raisin toast. You just don't know it.

LIV

There are many kinds of history. One kind is that which one reads about in books that chronicle the deeds of famous people and events. It feels strange to me to think of my own name showing up in one of those books someday in a chapter on Antarctic history. That was never really a part of what inspired or drove me. It makes me think of a poem by Antonio Machado that a friend of mine shared with me before I began my solo trek to the South Pole in 1994. Translated from its original Spanish, it reads:

> *Wanderer, the only way*
> *is your footsteps, there is no other.*
> *Wanderer, there is no way,*
> *you make the way as you go.*
> *As you go, you make the way*
> *and stopping to look behind,*
> *you see the path that your feet*
> *will never travel again.*
> *Wanderer, there is no way—*
> *only foam trails in the sea.*

We are so tiny in this universe; we each have to find our own way. It's a very difficult thing to find your purpose and meaning in this world. For me, the poem helps me think about how I approach making my own way in the world. I think it says that we should not be so concerned with making history. Our own steps determine our path, not the expectations of the world, or the backward glances of historians. So how does one decide which way to go? The same way that Ann and I have gotten through our own lives: by making it up as we go along, taking steps that feel right in our hearts.

I think there is another kind of history, though: the personal history that each of us carries around with us, our own record of ourselves and what has shaped us. To me, there is no question which kind of history I would rather be a part of. When I think about what I want my legacy to be, I think about Logan and the other children whose lives we touched. For many of them, our trip will be just a fun school project they look back on someday. But there are others for whom our expedition created one of those pivotal moments. I need look no further than the letters children have sent us to know that is true. I guess that makes me a better educator than explorer. I prefer it that way.

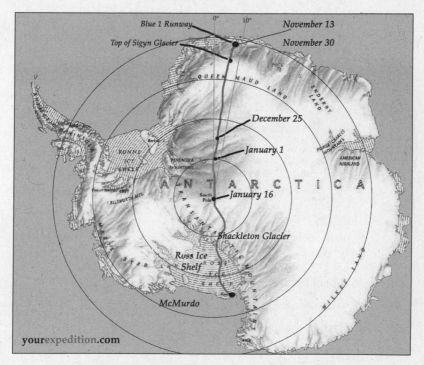

The Bancroft–Arnesen route across the Antarctic continent,
November 2000–February 2001.

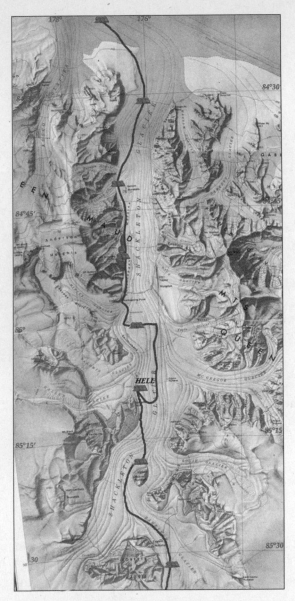

The Bancroft–Arnesen route down the Shackleton Glacier.

EPILOGUE

What follows are excerpts of interviews with people who were touched by or involved in Ann and Liv's expedition. Here, these people share how their contact with the historic trip affected them and their respective communities.

NORWAY

Per Visnes
Vice Principal (formerly)
Mølladammen School

More than four hundred children from this school followed Ann and Liv's expedition while exploring the topic of their own dreams with other schools across the world.

I first found out about the expedition from a notice in the newspaper in Norway. The article mentioned that Ann and Liv would be bringing equipment to communicate with the rest of the world. That use of technology sparked my interest because I saw a possibility for our students to follow the expedition and get a real time connection with these two during the trip.

What blossomed out of that first phone call to Liv was fantastic. I attended an international conference for educators with Ann and Liv, where I met other teachers interested in following the trek. We eventually had a global network of classrooms with students. Our idea was to create a way for these students to share their respective cultures and better understand what the world was like beyond their own front doors. During the expedition, we began exchanging e-mails with the other schools in which the children talked about their dreams, what they wanted to accomplish in life. Liv had already visited the school and shared with our students how her dream of going to Antarctica had begun a little before she was the age of our students, fourteen and fifteen.

The result was very interesting. This area, just outside Oslo, is fairly well off. Most of the children are from what I would call the upper class. Several of the children approached the assignment almost as a wish list, like winning the lottery. A few of them wrote that they dreamed of being rich someday. They were rather shocked when we got a letter from a boy their age living in the West Bank in a Palestinian village. His dream was to grow up and go to England to study and then return to his village and use his education for the benefit of the local society, to help change conditions there. It was a very different outlook on what young students could dream about and what their contribution to society could be. This boy's letter made our students reflect on their own values and, in many ways, gave them a chance to grow up a bit. I think they understood in a way that went beyond what we could have told them, how different the situation was for other children around the world.

TAIWAN

Yue-Chane Grace Hsing
Director
Taiwan School Net, a program that offers curriculum for local
teachers to download through an intranet.

*Roughly 10,000 students in Taiwan followed Ann and Liv's journey and took part
in the curriculum yourexpedition developed. The curriculum was translated into
Mandarin for grades K–12.*

The expedition really opened up Taiwanese students' vision. We live in the
tropics, so they don't see snow or ice. To them, Antarctica was a place
beyond their imagination. It also put them in touch with global issues and
children around the world. Just in Taiwan alone, at least forty school teachers got together regularly to talk about the curriculum and expedition, to
share how each of them was using it. There was such excitement. And for
the students, this project was so special and so unique—it is hard for us to
come up with another school curriculum that can compare!

For our society, Ann and Liv were a particular source of inspiration.
Before their trip began, our region suffered a terrible earthquake and many
of the children's schools were destroyed. But as we began to rebuild, we
would watch Ann and Liv on the ice and learn what we could from them
about overcoming difficulties. They are heroes to us.

From my point of view, this was not just an expedition. They connected their expedition to global education and used the Internet to distribute it across the world. This had never been done before! And to me it
was amazing that so many different places were able to use the same curriculum: Norway, South Africa, Canada, the United States.

The project also gave students a chance to think about their dreams
and how they might make them come true. Because we translated the curriculum, some students in Singapore and Hong Kong were also able to
join us in following the expedition. Our students talked to other children
in faraway places about their dreams. They came to know each other
through the *yourexpedition* Web site, and many of them are still in touch
with each other today.

I'm just so happy that we could be part of what Ann and Liv did. It was so much fun to read their e-mails every day and listen to their voices from the ice. Some of our teachers here in Taiwan were so inspired by the experience that they are planning to visit Antarctica soon. Ann and Liv and the people who worked with them created an opportunity for such a rich learning experience—it was the kind of lesson a teacher dreams of being able to share. Their journey was incredible and these children will never forget it.

UNITED STATES

Sarah Juncker
Teacher
Fairibault, Minnesota

One hundred kids in third, fourth, and fifth grades from four classrooms participated in a writing program in which the children wrote stories about Ann and Liv's expedition for their local newspaper. The project inspired the children to branch out from news writing to narrative writing which included writing poems and songs. Sarah Juncker's classroom was the one that Ann and Liv called from the Ross Ice Shelf after their decision to call for a pickup. Teachers Pat Otis, Deb Scheil, and Theresa Aldinger-Lauver also co-created the project.

I think because Antarctica is an "out-there" place, a place they've never seen or been, the project captured our kids' imaginations at once. It was also appealing because here were two women doing their thing, chasing their dreams, and kids are so naturally in tune with dreaming. Especially because they were two women, the girls were very excited. But the boys got into it as well. When they found out that Ann and Liv were pulling 250-pound sleds, they thought *that* was cool. They talked about how they hoped they'd be as tough as Ann and Liv when they grew up.

Each day, we would load up the *yourexpedition* Web site, get the update, and listen to Ann and Liv's reports. The kids couldn't wait to come to class to hear the news. Besides writing the news reporting and factual information about Antarctica for the newspaper, the children really turned those pages into a creative space. We would talk about coming up with a "golden line," something that one of the kids had written that was particularly evocative. Some poetry got thrown in from time to time. At one point, when the two women were stuck in a blizzard in their tent and not much was happening, one girl came up with the idea of rewriting the lyrics to a song. So she wrote a song telling how Ann and Liv used dental floss to repair their sails when they ran out of thread.

It was the first time many of the children had done something like this, writing and being published. They really understood that they were in a sense writing history, and they felt a strong connection to the historic expeditions of famous explorers. They understood that they were providing commentary on today's explorers.

And at the end—the phone call came. You can't imagine how excited the kids were. They had so much to say. They'd been writing about these two women for a year and felt such a connection to them. We had a speaker phone set up on a little brown stool in the center of the room, and all the kids were sitting on the floor around the phone. When we started the call, there was a space of about five feet between the phone and the first row of kids. But they were so excited, they just couldn't help themselves and they starting wriggling forward. About halfway into the conversation, these kids were just about on top of the phone! It was Valentine's Day, we were supposed to have a party, but kids said, "Who cares? Ann and Liv are calling today."

I'll never forget the minutes ticking by as the appointed time grew close, all of us staring at the phone. I was just thinking, please, please, please, let this work because the kids will be so disappointed if it doesn't come through. Then the phone rang. The looks on their faces were just unbelievable. I think the camera captured one little girl in the front row who just gasped and clasped her hands over her mouth. They couldn't believe it! It was Ann and Liv calling from Antarctica!

Hearing what the kids had to share with Ann and Liv was so touching for me. They had all made the connection right away between the expedition and the challenges that each of them faced. For Logan, the boy who gave such a heartfelt thank-you, the challenge was school itself. But by seeing the parallel to Ann and Liv's journey, he was able to accept that

that was okay; life is about challenge. In Ann and Liv, he found role models who pushed him to believe in himself. His expression of gratitude brought tears to everyone's eyes.

After that, it seemed as if Ann and Liv didn't want to get off the phone. There was such a pull from both sides: Please, let's keep talking. These kids reaching out for the contact that was making everything they'd done over the last year real and meaningful, and Ann and Liv reaching out for a living example of why they'd been through what they'd just been through. I didn't realize what the kids had done for Ann and Liv until much later. But in retrospect, I think Ann and Liv needed them as much as the kids needed Ann and Liv.

Afterward, when we hung up the phone, the kids were jumping up and down, whooping it up. Just incredibly happy.

I made arrangements to be part of the crowd that welcomed Ann and Liv at the airport in Minneapolis. I didn't want to be part of the mob scene, but I thought it was really important to thank them in person and tell them what they had done for my kids. Zoë and Charlie made sure that I actually got to talk to them, and that was when I found out how deeply we'd touched them, too. Ann did most of the talking. She took my hand and said, "You really don't know how much we needed that call." She has such intense eyes. I remember I was mesmerized listening to her. There was this intensity that emanated from her entire being. It was overwhelming just being in her presence.

The students who were third graders in that classroom are now in fifth grade. I see many of them in the hallways. And I sometimes talk to their teachers about their writing now. Of course, it's impossible to tell how much of the improvement they see in the kids' writing is related to this experience. But we definitely see that they are much more comfortable with the notion of themselves as writers—they carry notebooks and take on new writing assignments with relish. I think that seeing what they do now, I would have to believe that they are better students—and I would say just better people—for having had an experience like this that made them more aware of what's going on in the world, and inside of themselves.

SOUTH AFRICA

Liz Barrett
Teacher, formerly with Greenfield Girls Primary School in Cape
Town South Africa.

About 340 girls at Greenfield followed Ann and Liv's expedition and engaged in a
related curriculum about the continent. Close to 5,000 students in Cape Town fol-
lowed the expedition.

I stumbled across Ann and Liv's expedition site on the Internet, and when
I read that they planned to leave from Cape Town, I knew that I had to do
everything I could to persuade them to come and meet my girls. Children
love adventure and they love to learn. I believe that real learning comes
from finding out what sparks the group of children in your class and then,
as a teacher, you have to fan that fire of learning. You have to help children
to dream and to have fun while they're learning. The expedition was the
perfect opportunity to do just that.

The children were enthralled at their openness and honesty about the
expedition, their planning and the wonders of Antarctica. There have been
some explorers who tack on an educational program but for whom it's really
about the money and the glory and not about sharing the adventure and
inspiring children. Ann and Liv were the opposite. They were real and genuine, and the girls picked up on that straight away.

The kids were thrilled to meet Ann and Liv. Especially one girl in
my class who had a learning disability. Ann was so open about her own
dyslexia, and it was so apparent that she hadn't let it stop her from being
successful and happy. It was a life-changing experience for this girl. She
realized that her difference didn't have to control her life. It was suddenly
all right to be different, because she could still be a great person, like Ann.
And the girls were shattered [blown away] by the fact that Ann and Liv
were in their forties. I mean, these were women who could be their moth-
ers! I can tell you it made a lot of us teachers who were in our forties look
at ourselves a little differently after that as well.

Before Ann and Liv's visit, the kids had watched a documentary about an all-men's expedition to the Pole. And by the end of it, all the men hated each other, were making back-biting comments. They weren't really much of a team by the end of it. So when the girls met Ann and Liv, it was so obvious that they were a wonderful team and had such a great mental attitude. After they had left, the girls all said they would make it because they were so supportive of each other. They felt that this was a way that women would do expeditions better than men because they would help each other and cooperate.

Every day when the girls got to school, we would listen to the report that Ann and Liv had filed the previous day. These girls couldn't wait to come to school and hear from them. Having met Ann and Liv and getting to listen to their voices every day, the children felt as if the explorers were actually there. They felt a part of the expedition. In fact, they were quite worried for Ann and Liv at the end of the trip. I have no doubt that some of them had trouble sleeping over it. They had been watching weather conditions, and they were very scared that Ann and Liv wouldn't call for a plane, that they would try to tough it out. It caused huge stress among the kids. The girls were very aware of the danger of the winter closing in, and they were worried that the two of them might push it and be hurt or killed. We had watched all along and knew the risk. So all of us were very relieved when they decided to call for a plane. Some of the girls ventured that they didn't think Ann and Liv would have made that call if they'd been men. And the girls clearly thought that would've been a silly mistake.

It was a great lesson for the girls—how you don't always have control over everything, and how you have to deal with the situation that is, not the one you wish it could be.

THE GIRL SCOUTS

Dee Ebersole-Boukouzis
The Girl Scouts of the USA
Sports and Fitness Consultant

Through Girl Scouts of the USA, news of Ann and Liv's journey went out to 860,000 women and 2.7 million girls.

Charlie Hartwell and his team from *yourexpedition* approached us about a partnership in 1999, and we eventually worked together to create a patch project for the Girl Scouts. There was a natural fit between Girl Scouts and what we're about and what Ann and Liv were doing.

The patch project involved completing a workbook that covered everything from the technology Ann and Liv would need to the clothes they would wear and the route they would take. The girls could follow along on the Web site and get answers to their questions from the *yourexpedition* site. It was by far the largest participation we've ever had in a patch project—10,000 girls participated, which is more than twice our previous high in participation, and three times as many girls as patch projects typically draw. We discontinued the patch project in May 2002, and still had scout leaders and scouts asking for it more than a year after Ann and Liv's journey was over!

Why was it such a huge success? Well, I think Ann and Liv were uniquely inspiring because they were (and are) so earnest in their endeavor. It was never about making money or getting press for them. They were incredibly genuine. You could tell that they genuinely cared about the girls and their dreams. People, both kids and adults, responded to that. And I think the fact that the girls were able to follow Ann and Liv "live" as the two crossed Antarctica was also key. It was a real drama unfolding for the girls as they checked into the Internet every day. And although we had 10,000 girls trying to earn patches, I'm sure we had many more troops just following the expedition for the fun of it.

We're approached by hundreds of people every year wanting access to our audience. We are very picky about whom we associate with. But there is no question that we'll continue our relationship with Ann and Liv. We need everyday heroes. Even the adult scout leaders related to these women in their forties as they pursued their dreams. There just aren't a lot of powerful female role models out there, and these two are it. Their strength of character—and when I say this I mean their mental and physical strength—and their use of that strength not to further themselves but to help others are just astounding. There are many professional athletes out there who could not care less about being role models for kids. These two really care about kids and inspiring them. That is their mission.

ASSOCIATES

Fred Haberman and Sarah Bell Haberman
Founders, Haberman and Associates, Ann and Liv's public relations firm.

The story of Ann and Liv's journey was told worldwide in the press, garnering attention from the likes of David Letterman and Daryn Kagan of CNN. All told, the publications and shows in which the expedition appeared had combined audiences of 2.3 billion.

SARAH: Why did this expedition spark people's imagination? To bring it to a philosophical level, the journey was the quintessential hero's journey. These were two modern-day heroes who took a myth that we all relate to and brought it to life. When you tell that story well, it touches a chord in human beings.

FRED: And because it was a hero's journey, it had incredible emotional appeal. We found that top journalists from around the world—whether from CNN or the BBC, whether Katie Couric or Daryn Kagan—were compelled to cover the story because they were touched by it individually. CNN interrupted its ongoing political coverage of the standoff on the presidential race to talk to Ann and Liv! I think it was notable that the journalists themselves, who are typically a pretty skeptical audience, were inspired as well.

For me personally, what was inspiring about Ann and Liv was that they were ordinary people doing something extraordinary. They don't have the ego, that aura of self-importance. They're the type of individuals who, when you were running the half-mile race in seventh grade, would come out of nowhere to win the race and afterwards accept the award and give credit to somebody else. They never lost perspective; even though they had so many opportunities to bask in this limelight, they always gave it to someone else.

SARAH: I think their real appeal is the authenticity that they exude—parents, kids, reporters—they all pick up on something when it is real.

Because of that authenticity, they managed to forge this deep connection with people of all ages, races, nationalities, gender. They reminded people of the dreams they had when they were twelve years old, and the wonder and excitement that brings—and that it is never too late to pursue those dreams. I believe that, because of what Ann and Liv accomplished, there are people out there who have awakened to what they are passionate about in life, and they're going to go after it.

THE COMPANY

John Tuttle
Vice President of Technology
yourexpedition

I had no idea how big this was going to get, how many people all over the world were going to latch on to the expedition. We had some traffic on our Web site about six months before the expedition started. A news story would run and it would increase a bit. We put the online curriculum up and that generated some interest. But honestly? I thought we would get some interest from Canada and Norway, and of course the United States. But I didn't have enough experience with Internet word of mouth to predict anything more. Charlie was saying, "We could touch millions, blah, blah, blah." But Charlie talks like that all the time. It's that visionary thing he does.

So we translated the online curriculum into Mandarin—and whoa! There was a spike. Then Ann and Liv began attending educational conferences. All of a sudden we had people from ten, fifteen countries visiting the site. That's when it began to dawn on me that this was going to be huge. Teachers were talking to teachers. The day Ann and Liv departed Cape Town, the numbers went through the roof. We went from 500 people a day to 10,000 people a day. Then the first CNN story hit and we crashed our host server.

And the mail! We didn't even have a place on the site originally for people to email Ann and Liv. But people were writing to them directly in the comment box that was for the site administrator—me. So we put up a link to email to Ann and Liv. Pretty soon we were getting a hundred messages a day. Our biggest day was about four hundred letters—in a *single* day. And the majority of it was meaty stuff in which kids, teachers, and Girl Scouts were pouring out their hearts saying, we're following, we're watching, you're inspiring us. And I thought, "This is amazing!"

Stan and I had put a route map up on the site, and we would post Ann and Liv's location, giving all the geeky coordinates. We started getting e-mails from navigation clubs and orienteering circles: "Hey, you're wrong. You're off by 100 yards." I'm, like, hey, we just want a rough idea of where they are; we're not trying to drop Christmas presents on their sled from an airplane. Relax. Then we just kinda rode it. I stopped counting after we hit forty-three countries.

I think one of the biggest reasons people connected with this journey was that they could hear Ann and Liv making it. When you downloaded their daily reports, they were talking to you. They weren't going on about their location and equipment. They had a thought for the day, or they talked honestly about the pulling and how hard it was. Their honesty created a connection for anyone who hooked into it. You weren't watching somebody at a news desk or someone with a microphone interpreting it. It was straight from them. We felt that every day we were getting confirmation from our audience about how much of a difference the trip was making to them. You'd get e-mail from someone who'd say that he had just lost his legs in an accident, he's going through physical therapy, and reading about Ann and Liv was what made him want to get out of bed that day. That was something.

The journey has definitely changed *me* forever, too: how I view group dynamics, how I look at what is possible, how I face adversity. Is there an unsolvable problem? Probably, but there is a lot you can do before it gets that far. I'm really glad just to be here in this job working for this company—for the reasons that it lets me contribute, step out of my role when it's warranted, and do so many other little things that I appreciate. I just feel very lucky to have fallen into this wonderful situation. Somebody once asked me before I got this job, "What do you aspire to do?" And one of my goals was that I wanted to love going to work. I didn't know what that meant and had no idea what that included at the time. But I found it here. And that is a realized dream. I see how many people are unhappy doing what they're doing, and how it taints everything around them. I want more than that. I want my kids to have careers that make them feel fulfilled. I don't want them to have a huge separation between who they are at work and who they are. And I want that for me, too.

Stan Oleson
General Counsel
yourexpedition

I think for me, one of the most powerful aspects of being part of the expedition was the sense of connectedness I had with a larger community.

I wrote a regular e-mail newsletter for our audience, called "From the Sled." I'd hit "send," and it would go out to a couple of thousand people. One of the first times I sent it out, I got e-mail back about five minutes later from a woman working at the South Pole. We wrote back and forth during the course of the day. She was a lawyer on leave who decided to work at the Pole. We wound up chatting about how much we both enjoyed being lawyers and the importance of trying to do something meaningful with our work. The fact that I was corresponding with someone on the other side of the world really blew me away—as did the fact that we had so much in common. And it was a different view of the "epiphanies" that the journey was inspiring. It wasn't the case of someone headed West and then hearing about Ann and Liv made them go East; it was just a bit of reinforcement that the path she was on, and the one that I was on, were the right ones for each of us.

In one of our daily Web updates, I wrote about what Ann and Liv were eating on the ice, and mentioned that they each ate a can of potato chips each day. The next day, we got e-mail from Uzbekistan from a couple of kids, who wrote, "We don't have potato chips in Uzbekistan, but we know what they are like. How do you keep them from crumbling?" That just tickled me—that we were reaching someone so far removed, both geographically and culturally from what I was familiar with. How cool that a little thing like curiosity about potato chips could start a conversation across continents and oceans! Of course, I wrote back to them right away: "We don't have many rules around here at *yourexpedition*, but one of them is that we answer all mail from Uzbekistan."

For me personally, that sense of community and connectedness came at a really important time in my life. Right before Liv joined the team, we all went up to Charlie's cabin for a weekend and each of us drew pictures or maps of our own personal expeditions. I think at the time, the title of my journey was "Middle-aged, but Not Dead." That seemed a lot less funny a few weeks later when I got the cancer diagnosis. But I think the great thing about having taken this job at *yourexpedition* before I had that struggle, having left a safer, more predictable job before I knew that I had cancer, was that I had already made an important commitment in my life to stop coasting. And it didn't take a crisis for me to figure that out, though being ill sure did underscore the importance of that choice.

I did have that one proverbial night of re-examining my life, thinking about what I wished I'd done differently. And there weren't many things I wanted to change. Not many regrets. And that felt good. That's something I'm not sure you can examine honestly until you're in a position where you can't bullshit yourself anymore. But in that one night of clarity, I felt like I had a broader view of my life and choices. I could see the convergence around following dreams and less-safe choices. I guess the overwhelming feeling that came out of that was thinking, "I never want to waste a day again." I'm sure that I do still waste time, get derailed in unimportant things or lose the sense of wonder. But I'm more aware of it, and hopefully I snap out of it faster than I used to. That was an important lesson for me from my own personal expedition.

Charlie Hartwell
President
yourexpedition

My big "a-ha" moment was when I met Ann and a business plan popped into my head. I knew this expedition was going to be big. But never did I think we'd reach 3 million kids in sixty-five countries. I had so many moments when the "bigness" of what we were doing caught up with me:

I was driving to work at three in the morning and listening to NPR at one of the crucial moments of the expedition when I heard a report from the BBC guy who was on the ship going to meet Ann and Liv at McMurdo. That was just unbelievable, knowing that report was being heard all over the world. A friend of mine wrote from Angola to say that he had seen coverage of the expedition on CNN. Time and time again, I kept having this realization of how in crossing a huge, frozen continent, these two women had made the world so small. Kids in Taiwan, South Africa, Norway, Brazil, Ecuador—they were all following the expedition and talking about their dreams with us and each other as if we all lived in the same place.

But you only have to watch the way kids react to Ann and Liv in person once to understand why that happened. I've seen kids, some of whom have no more than a seven-minute attention span for anything that isn't Nintendo, sit during one of Ann's speeches for forty-five minutes, riveted, hanging onto every word. There is something they respond to in her, and in Liv, that is just instinctive.

I think that connection is pretty amazing because of how different Ann and Liv are from kids' typical role models. Many kids like and idolize Michael Jordan. But most kids understand that they're never going to *be* Michael Jordan. That's a fantasy, unreal. Ann and Liv are real. And the things that they aspired to do they accomplished with a lot of talent and skill, but also with something available to the rest of us: determination and belief.

Anne Atwood
Director of Sponsorship
yourexpedition

I was definitely affected by the journey as an individual. I grew and learned a lot, especially from Ann. I remember her telling me about how after she had made the trip to the North Pole in 1986, the first woman to do that, she figured out that she had a responsibility to all other women. She told me that at a book launch in New York for *Remarkable Women of the 20th Century,* in which she was featured along with Gloria Steinem. I realized as I watched her give a speech that night that there really is a responsibility for women across the world to continue to share their stories and become role models—and not even just for women, but for men, too. A responsibility to say, "I did this and I'm this tall and I had no funding and I did this." I guess what I mean is that we are caretakers for the dreams of the future generation, women and men. And how can they possibly do all they're capable of doing if we don't constantly share our own stories of triumph, challenges, and failure? There is something very important in storytelling that is critical to our younger generation. Sharing those stories makes a huge difference. Before I started this job, I didn't realize that. But that is what this expedition has been in our own way—part of a movement to create change.

THE BANCROFT–ARNESEN EXPEDITION EQUIPMENT LIST

EQUIPMENT

1 Hilleberg Keron 3-person tent with extra poles and stakes
Emergency, one-person, bivvy shelter for repairs
2 Mountain Hardwear sleeping bags, 2 pads, and 2 bivvy sacks
2 Fjellpulken AS sleds
2 Harnesses
2 Pair titanium towbars

8 Fischer sails:
- two 4 sq. meter storm sails
- two 11 sq. meter sail
- two 15 sq. meter sail w/flap
- two 32 sq. meter NASA sail wing

2 pair K2 sailing skis
2 pair Madshus pulling skis
2 pair Mødre ski boots (custom design)
2 pair Granite Gear telecuffs
2 pair Swix poles
2 spare poles
4 pair Ascension nylon ski skins
Ski skin glue

Flags (Norway, USA, South Africa, Australia, Tibet)
Tibetan prayer shawl

CLIMBING EQUIPMENT

1 lightweight shovel
1 55 cm Grivel ice axe/hammer
2 30-meter lengths of rope
4 titanium ice screws
2 pulleys
2 jumars
2 snow anchors
2 pair crampons
8 carabiners

TECHNOLOGY/COMMUNICATIONS

2 Magellan 315 handheld GPS
Argos transmitter
* Magellan GSC satellite text messaging communication device
2 Suunto global needle compasses
2 Suunto watches X-Lander and Vector with altimeter, barometer, and
   compass
2 anemometers
* 1 satellite phone
* 2 Motorola Talkabout T289 two-way radios
* Apple Powerbook G3 laptop computer
* Sony Mini DV camera with lapel microphone
Yashica camera
Nikon 35T camera
Minox camera
Solar panel
Centigrade/Fahrenheit thermometer
Continuum crank
Batteries, *back-up battery charger, cords, film
Maps, aerial photos and charts
*equipment adapted to be solar charged

REPAIR KIT

Leatherman multi-purpose tool
Ski binding parts
Sewing kit (material, needles, etc.)
Spare stove parts
Wire
Duct tape
Spare sled pieces (screws, etc.)
Zipper heads
Spare sail parts
Link joint for tent repair
Parachute cord
Epoxy glue

PERSONAL ITEMS (PER PERSON)

Lotion
Moist wipes
Toothpaste, toothbrush, dental floss
Knife
Lighter, storm-proof matches
Sun block protection, lip protection
Book, journal, pens
Postcards to send from the South Pole
1 pair knee braces
University of Minnesota research questionnaire

CLOTHING AND ACCESSORIES

Norrøna Gore Tex jacket, pants
Long underwear tops, bottoms, and underwear (Brynje, Devold, Patagonia)
Patagonia pile tops
Down: jacket, vest, pants, booties
Socks: liner, wicking, vapor barrier, wool
Windstopper hats (sailing), wool hats (pulling), balaclava hat, ear muffs

Neoprene facemasks
Mittens, gloves, wristlets
Bollé glacier glasses
Carrera goggles with face protector
Steger Mukluks

KITCHEN

Five 1.5 liter thermos bottles
One 3-liter insulated cook pot, "The Willy Pot"
Two MSR XGKII stoves with platform
White gas, 30 liters
20 Sigg fuel bottles, capacity 1.5 liters
2 Nalgene 32 oz. water bottles
2 bowls, 2 thermal mugs, 2 spoons
Kitchen bag: (spices, lighter, matches, whisk broom)
Toilet paper

SAMPLE MENU

Breakfast:
   2 mugs each of coffee/cocoa drink
   A bowl of oatmeal with nuts, dried fruit, and a tablespoon of oil
Lunch:
   1 200 gram Chocolate bar each
   1 high energy bar each
   Almonds or cashews
   Hot sport drink
Dinner:
   1 cup of soup each
   1 6.5 oz. can crushed Pringles each
   1 pouch of Real Turmat dinner each (fish and potatoes and pasta
      were our favorite flavors)
   Mugs of cocoa or tea

MEDICAL KIT

Zithromycin–general antibiotic, lung and urinary tract infection
Duracef–general antibiotic, especially for skin infections
Cipro–antibiotic
Fucidin cream–antibiotic/skin infections
Fluconazole–yeast infection
Lanzo–dyspepsia or side effects from other drugs
Immodium–anti diarrheal
Vicoidin ES–narcotic for significant pain
Celebrex–anti-inflamatory/pain managment
Dispril–pain killer for frostbite
Petidin suppository–strong pain killer
Persantin–severe frostbite
Tylenol ES–mild pain
Spersadex–eyedrops
Kloramf–eye cream for infection
Tobrex Ophthalmologic–eye scratches or snowblindness
Silvadene Ointment–burns and frostbite
Labiosan–lip protection
Zinc oxide cream–lip and face protection
Dermabond–sterile skin adhesive
Betadine skin preps
Alcohol pads
Hydrocortisone cream
A&D cream
Gauze pads in various sizes
Gauze roll
First aid tape
Ace bandage
Band-Aid adhesive bandages
Ear plugs

ACKNOWLEDGMENTS

ANN AND LIV

A very special thanks to our collaborator and writer, **Cheryl Dahle,** for giving clear voice to our story. Cheryl helped put order to our thoughts and experiences, all the while infusing her deep understanding of our passion for the remote and fragile ice of Antarctica.

We are deeply indebted to the corporate sponsors and champions whose belief in us and monetary or in-kind support made our trip possible. These people brought a passion to their roles in our expedition that was certainly equal to that of the visionaries in history who funded Shackleton's ships or invested in Amundsen's dog teams. Thanks to Hans-Olov Olsson, Sören Johansson, Roger Ormisher, Thomas Andersson, and Kjell Bergh at **Volvo Cars Worldwide**. At **Pfizer Pharmaceuticals**, special thanks to Barbara Gerolimatos, Ruth Merkatz, Fredrik Bendiksen, David Helgans, and Rebecca Tillet. At **Motorola,** our gratitude to John Cipolla, John Melby, Corrine Miller, and Dave Weisz. We are deeply grateful to Steve Wilhite and Suzanne Lindbergh of **Apple Computer.** Thanks also to Jeff Farmer of **Continuum Control;** Michael Cookson of **Get Real Girl.**

We were privileged to strike partnerships with organizations who deeply affected our ability to reach children with our education message. We are particularly grateful to Dee Ebersole-Boukouzis, Verna Simpkins of the **Girl**

Scouts of the USA, as well as all the Girl Scout troops. Lynne Whitt and Teresa Stahl of the **National Center For Health Education.**

For in-kind donations of equipment and supplies, we thank: Doctors Steve Sterner, Jeff Ho, and Bill Heegaard of **HCMC;** Dr. Nina Lindstad in Norway, who helped assemble the first aid kit; Bill Wheelehan, Guy Rudisill, and Ed Aymar of the **United States Armed Forces,** who generously donated satellite phones and universal chips; to **Rottefella** for ski bindings; **Swix** for ski poles; **Madshus** for skis; **Fjellpulken** for our sleds; **Teamtrade AS** for titanium bars; **Hotel Finse 1222** in Norway for accommodations during our training; **Alfa Skofabrikk** for our ski boots; **Stibolt-Norge Ski AS** for our ropes, crampons, and carabiners; **REAL Turmat** and **Drytech** for our dehydrated meals on the ice; **Freia,** our chocolate provider; **Stan Ryan** for our cooking oil; **Phil Stringer** for GU; **Hilleberg** for our tunnel tent, **Grain Millers** for our oatmeal and **Norrøna** for our jackets; thanks also to **Framkomiteen, Mountain Hardwear,** and Hans Clausen **Invest AS.** Simon Foster of **Simon Delivers,** who lent walk-in freezer space to test our technological equipment.

Several individuals used their skills and talents to help us build or customize unique equipment and gear for our expedition. We are indebted to them for their collaboration and craftsmanship: **Bjørn Nordstrøm** made our titanium tow bars; **Jan Martinussen** arranged the purchase of titanium; **Nils Finsrud** designed and constructed our sail harnesses; **Steinar Børke** designed and crafted custom knives and also built the metal link from titanium tow bars to the harnesses; **Eva Fischer,** who helped design and sewed all of our sails; ski-sailors **Arve Roaas, Sigurd Parmann,** and **Morten Svatun,** who offered advice and consultation.

Thanks to the individuals whose support and professionalism made our trip easier: **Arne Storhaug,** manager Hotel Finse 1222; **Pål Olimb** of Alfa Ski Boots; **Torbjørn Ragg** of Rottefella; **Lars Hanstad** of Madshus; **David Durkan** of Stibolt Norge Ski AS; **Anne Rustadstuen** of Fjellpulken; **Rolf Hansen** of Drytech.

Deepest thanks to friends and loved ones whose personal gifts lifted our spirits and "spoiled us" on and off the ice: **Peg Murray,** who gave us Cinema Toffee; **Sue Giller,** who gave us Scotch; **Jan Arnold,** who contributed gourmet cocoa; **Berit Arnesen,** who baked her special Kentucky Cake; **Alicia**

Gutierrez, who knit gloves for us; Randi B. Noyes, who donated wine; and Ruth Ann Brown, who gave us gear. Octavio Ruiz and Ron "Bear" Cronick for their big medicine and prayers.

This trip would not have been possible without the tireless efforts of the yourexpedition *crew and a wider team of external supporters:* Charlie Hartwell: your vision, energy, and passion were the heart of this expedition. Thank you. Our love and thanks to the whole *yourexpedition* team: Anne Atwood, John Tuttle, Stan Oleson, Kristi Russo, Steve Rosengren, Carolee Lindsey, Lee Lyon, Susan Zarambo, and Mary Wagner. Special thanks to Zöe Alderfer Ryan, former *yourexpedition* team member who was the point person for the education program. Thanks also to other *yourexpedition* team members who joined us for part of the journey: Randal Dietrich, Neal Kielar, Beth Gipsky, Nick Reti, and Eric Madsen.

To Haberman and Associates, our close partners in this odyssey: Desire to share our story is only the first step to making it happen. Your skill and dedication in presenting our journey to the world ensured that we reached millions of children, teachers, and others willing to come along. Thanks, Fred Haberman and Sarah Bell Haberman, Liz Morris Otto, Suzanne Fedoruk, Molly Gaines, Carol Schuler, and Brian Wachtler.

Special thanks to Congressman Jim Ramstad for help securing the satellite phone; to Gedney Tuttle for help with the same; to Mike Wright, of Super Valu, our champion; to Mariko Miyamoto, our personal assistant and lifesaver in Cape Town; to the Sir Huey team and Michael Cohen; to Sir Charles Swithinbank for information on the Shackleton Glacier; to Katy Jensen, of South Pole Station and our gracious host; to John Lindsay of Oregon Public Broadcasting; to Børge Ousland, Lars Ebbesen, and Jan Erling Haugland for advice and inspiration; to Ulf S. H. Christiansen, former Consulate General for Norway in Minneapolis; to Inger Tallaksen of the NACC; to Paul Røer; to Diana and Stein Hoff; to Marv Mikesh, who ignited the international education program; to Christi Mack, a champion who opened door and hearts for us; to Kathy Flynn, Elena Gandia, and Mary Palmer Lilly, volunteers who helped answer our fans' e-mail and lent a hand in the *yourexpedition* offices; to **Lanie van Reenen and staff** of the Welgelegen Guest House in Cape Town.

Warmest thanks to: **John and Lucy Hartwell, David Hartwell,** and **Elizabeth DeBaut, Jill and Tim Geoffrion, Jeff and Lucy Heegaard, Randy Sukovich, Joanne Kletscher, Donna Schmitz, George Appleby.** Also to **Robin Hartwell,** for supporting Charlie's dream to build something unique. Our Advisory Board: **Rick Gentile, Bo Ewald, Steve Bohlig, Rob Hawthorne, Yue-Chane Grace Hsing, Steve Inch, Inge Lise Hammer, Ed Villaume, Clay Yonce, Mike Benson, John Taylor, Keith Woods, Veronica Sive, Annemarie Osborne, Jack Stanton.**

Thanks to **Adventure Network International** for safe transport to the continent and pick-up on the Ross Ice Shelf. Our gratitude as well to **Don and Margie McIntyre,** owners of *Sir Hubert Wilkins,* and the crew.

For their advocacy and dedication in making this book a reality, we thank **Laureen Rowland,** our literary agent with The David Black Agency and **Marnie Cochran,** our editor with Da Capo Press.

ANN WOULD LIKE TO PERSONALLY ACKNOWLEDGE

Mom and Dad, for nurturing all my wild dreams. **Bill, Hunter, Carrie, Sarah**—my forever-supportive siblings. **Andrew Bancroft-Howard,** my trainer. **Alma, Maya, Morgan, Saman,** and **Frank** for painting my pulling skis. **Greg Steiver, Jeff Heegaard, Fred Haberman,** and **Sarah Bell Haberman**—you helped me to articulate the obvious. Also: **Will Steger,** who gave me my start to the big ones. **Greg Lais, Jan Malcolm, Kris Carlton, Rhonda Grider and Family,** and **the AWE Family,** for laying the foundation to this expedition and much more.

LIV WOULD LIKE TO PERSONALLY ACKNOWLEDGE

Einar, my best friend, training partner, discussing partner, and the love of my life. **Mom and Dad,** thanks for a childhood with outdoor life, storytelling, and books that created all the wild dreams. **Jannicke, Linn,** and **Birgitte**—thank you for your great support, love, and friendship. **Sigmund,** my supportive brother.

CHERYL

My profound thanks to my collaborators, Ann and Liv. I feel graced by the trust they extended in sharing with me the innermost details of their lives and journey. I've been honored to help tell the story of two such inspiring women who have made a significant difference in the world. John, Stan, Anne, and Charlie—thanks for enduring my endless interviewing and subjective judgments on "round" faces and such with patience and good humor.

I am indebted to numerous friends and colleagues who gave feedback as this manuscript evolved: John Dahle Jr., Fara Warner, Andrew Stevenson, Kevin F. Sherry, Lisa Baird, Denise Armstrong, Brent Mitchell, Alison Overholt, and Kimberly DaSilva. Special thanks to my dear teacher and mentor Sarah Robbins, who provided her invaluable insights as well. Without her guidance many years ago, I would never have had the courage to become a writer at all.

I owe much to my family and loved ones: to my mother for her love, support and astounding generosity; to my father for his encouragement and permission to make my own rules; to my "chosen family"—you know who you are—I am blessed by your presence in my life

Thank you to friends who provided emotional support above and beyond the call of duty during the writing process: Tony Rodriguez, Alex Zuccarelli, Georgina Ritchie, Dawn Wells Nadeau, and my brother, John.

And sincerest thanks to Laureen Rowland—friend, agent, sounding board, editor, and guardian of my sanity. You rock, chica. I look forward to our future collaborations.

ABOUT *YOUREXPEDITION*

Ann and Liv remain close to many of the children, teachers, and other followers from around the world whom they touched throughout their Antarctic trek. The women continue their work of inspiring people to pursue dreams and provide guidance to help others succeed in life's "expeditions"—whether those journeys take place in the frozen wilderness, in the classroom, or in the boardroom. Through their twelve-person company *yourexpedition*, based in Minneapolis, Minnesota, Ann and Liv share their expedition stories and images. The Bancroft Arnesen Explore programs include corporate motivational products as well as books, films, and presentations. They also have a children's book titled *Ann and Liv Cross Antarctica: A Dream Come True!* for ages seven through twelve. You can read more about Ann and Liv's current adventures at www.yourexpedition.com.

FOR THE BEST IN PAPERBACKS, LOOK FOR THE

In every corner of the world, on every subject under the sun, Penguin represents quality and variety—the very best in publishing today.

For complete information about books available from Penguin—including Penguin Classics, Penguin Compass, and Puffins—and how to order them, write to us at the appropriate address below. Please note that for copyright reasons the selection of books varies from country to country.

In the United States: Please write to *Penguin Group (USA), P.O. Box 12289 Dept. B, Newark, New Jersey 07101-5289* or call 1-800-788-6262.

In the United Kingdom: Please write to *Dept. EP, Penguin Books Ltd, Bath Road, Harmondsworth, West Drayton, Middlesex UB7 0DA.*

In Canada: Please write to *Penguin Books Canada Ltd, 10 Alcorn Avenue, Suite 300, Toronto, Ontario M4V 3B2.*

In Australia: Please write to *Penguin Books Australia Ltd, P.O. Box 257, Ringwood, Victoria 3134.*

In New Zealand: Please write to *Penguin Books (NZ) Ltd, Private Bag 102902, North Shore Mail Centre, Auckland 10.*

In India: Please write to *Penguin Books India Pvt Ltd, 11 Panchsheel Shopping Centre, Panchsheel Park, New Delhi 110 017.*

In the Netherlands: Please write to *Penguin Books Netherlands bv, Postbus 3507, NL-1001 AH Amsterdam.*

In Germany: Please write to *Penguin Books Deutschland GmbH, Metzlerstrasse 26, 60594 Frankfurt am Main.*

In Spain: Please write to *Penguin Books S. A., Bravo Murillo 19, 1° B, 28015 Madrid.*

In Italy: Please write to *Penguin Italia s.r.l., Via Benedetto Croce 2, 20094 Corsico, Milano.*

In France: Please write to *Penguin France, Le Carré Wilson, 62 rue Benjamin Baillaud, 31500 Toulouse.*

In Japan: Please write to *Penguin Books Japan Ltd, Kaneko Building, 2-3-25 Koraku, Bunkyo-Ku, Tokyo 112.*

In South Africa: Please write to *Penguin Books South Africa (Pty) Ltd, Private Bag X14, Parkview, 2122 Johannesburg.*